KU-070-599

GEM

SPANISH

PHRASE BOOK

COLLINS
London and Glasgow

First published 1986

Consultant
Alicia de Benito

ISBN 0 00 459404-5

Other Travel Gem
Phrase Books:

French

German

Italian

Your **Travel Gem** Phrase Book will prove an invaluable companion on your holiday or trip abroad. In a genuinely handy format, it gives you all you need to say for basic communication, with fast and direct alphabetical access to the relevant information. Be sure to pack it with your passport!

Its layout provides two means of quick alphabetical access:

> 99 practical topics arranged in A-to-Z order from ACCOMMODATION to WINTER SPORTS via such topics as MENUS, ROOM SERVICE and TAXIS. Each topic gives you the basic phrases you will need, and in many cases an additional list with useful extra words. Just flick through the pages to the topic you need to look up;

> an alphabetical index at the back - WORDS - listing up to 1400 key words found in the 99 topics, for fast access to words which do not immediately seem to belong to a particular topic (such as 'safety pin, lose, passport').

This way you have the possibility of browsing through topics, as in more traditional phrase books, as well as having the advantage of alphabetical listing. The best of both worlds.

For information on GRAMMAR, PRONUNCIATION, the ALPHABET or CONVERSION CHARTS, , just flick through the pages until you get to that topic in alphabetical order. Though **Travel Gems** do not assume prior knowledge of the foreign language, some basic facts about grammar will help you improvise and get more out of your conversations with local people.

Whenever relevant, travel information has been included. Some likely replies to what you might say have also been shown in several topics (such as DENTIST or DOCTOR).

Enjoy your stay!

You should carry a red warning triangle in case of breakdowns or accidents.

There's been an accident Ha habido un accidente
a a-beedo oon akthee-den-te

I've crashed my car He chocado
e cho-kado

Can I see your insurance certificate please? ¿Me enseña el seguro de su coche, por favor?
me en-senya el se-gooro de soo ko-che, por fa-bor

We will have to report it to the police Tendremos que dar parte a la policía
ten-dremos ke dar par-te a la polee-thee-a

We should call the police Deberíamos llamar a la policía
de-beree-amos lyamar a la polee-thee-a

He ran into me Se me echó encima
se me e-cho en-theema

I ran into him Choqué contra él
cho-ke kontra el

He was driving too fast El iba demasiado rápido
el eeba dema-syado ra-peedo

He was too close El iba demasiado cerca
el eeba dema-syado therka

He did not give way No cedió el paso
no thedyo el paso

The car number was ... La matrícula del coche era ...
la matree-koola del ko-che era ...

He was coming from my right/left Venía por la derecha/izquierda
benee-a por la de-recha/eeth-kyerda

damage
los desperfectos
desper-fektos

documents
los documentos
dokoo-mentos

driving licence
el permiso de conducir
per-meeso de kondoo-theer

green card
la carta verde
karta ber-de

insurance company
la compañía de seguros
kompa-nyee-a de se-gooros

law
la ley
le-ee

lawyer
el abogado
abo-gado

offence
la infracción
eenfrak-thyon

police station
la comisaría (de policía)
komee-saree-a (de polee-thee-a)

See also EMERGENCIES

Before you set off it is advisable to obtain proper medical and accident insurance. Ambulances have to be paid for: the emergency operator will tell you which number to dial.

There has been an accident Ha habido un accidente *a a-beedo oon akthee-den-te*	**bandage** la venda *benda*
Call an ambulance/a doctor Llame a una ambulancia/a un médico *lya-me a oona amboo-lanthya/a oon me-deeko*	**bitten** mordido *mordee-do*
He has hurt himself Se ha hecho daño *se a e-cho danyo*	**dead** muerto *mwerto*
I am hurt Me he hecho daño *me e e-cho danyo*	**dislocate, to** dislocarse *deeslo-kar-se*
He is seriously injured/bleeding Está gravemente herido/Está sangrando *esta gra-be-men-te e-reedo/esta san-grando*	**hospital** el hospital *ospee-tal*
He can't breathe/move No puede respirar/moverse *no pwe-de respee-rar/mober-se*	**serious** grave *gra-be*
I can't move my arm/leg No puedo mover el brazo/la pierna *no pwedo mober el bratho/la pyerna*	**slip, to** resbalar *resba-lar*
Cover him up Cúbrale *koobra-le*	**sprain** la torcedura *tor-thedoo-ra*
Don't move him No le mueva *no le mweba*	**stung** picado *pee-kado*
He has broken his arm/cut himself Se ha roto el brazo/Se ha cortado *se a roto el bratho/se a kor-tado*	**sunburn** la quemadura del sol *kema-doora del sol*
I have had a fall Me he caído *me e ka-eedo*	**sunstroke** la insolación *eenso-lathyon*

See also HOTEL DESK, ROOM SERVICE, SELF-CATERING
Hotels are grouped into categories of from one to five stars, and
boarding houses (*pensiones* and *hostales*) are graded one, two or
three stars. You can also stay at *paradores nacionales*, often
converted historical buildings in beautiful settings, and *albergues
de carretera*, set at strategic points on main roads and motorways.

I want to reserve a single/double room
Quiero reservar una habitación
individual/doble
*kye*ro re-ser*bar* oona abee-tath*yon*
eendee-beed*wal*/*do-ble*

With bath/shower Con baño/ducha
kon *banyo*/*doocha*

**Do you have facilities for the
disabled?** ¿Tienen ustedes instalaciones
especiales para los minusválidos?
tye-nen oos-*te*-des eensta-lathyo-nes es-
peth*ya*-les para los meenoos-*balee*-dos

I want bed and breakfast/full board
Quiero habitación y desayuno/pensión
completa
*kye*ro abee-tath*yon* ee desa-*yoo*no/
pensyon kom*pleta*

What is the daily/weekly rate? ¿Cuál es
la tarifa por día/por semana?
kwal es la ta-*reefa* por *dee*-a/por se-*mana*

**I want to stay three nights/from ...
till...** Quiero quedarme tres noches/del ...
al ...
*kye*ro ke*dar*-me tres *no*-ches/del ... al ...

We'll be arriving at 7 p.m. Llegaremos a
las siete de la tarde
lyega-*remos* a las *sye*-te de la *tar*-de

Shall I confirm by letter? ¿Quiere que
lo confirme por escrito?
kye-re ke lo konfeer-me por es*cree*-to

balcony
el balcón
balkon

bathroom
el cuarto de baño
kwarto de *banyo*

double bed
la cama de
matrimonio
kama de matree-
monyo

evening meal
la cena
thena

half-board
la media pensión
medya pensyon

lift
el ascensor
as-then*sor*

lunch
el almuerzo
al*mwer*-tho

single bed
la cama individual
kama eendee-
beed*wal*

youth hostel
el albergue de
juventud
alber-ge de
khooben*tood*

Where do I check in for the flight to Milan? ¿Dónde tengo que facturar para el vuelo de Milán?
*don-de **tengo** ke faktoo-**rar** para el **bwelo** de **meelan***

I'd like an aisle seat/a window seat Querría un asiento al lado del pasillo/un asiento con ventanilla
*kerree-a oon **asyen**-to al **lado** del pasee-lyo/oon **asyen**-to kon benta-**neel**ya*

Will a meal be served on the plane? ¿Servirán una comida en el avión?
*serbee-**ran** oona **komee**-da en el **abyon***

Where is the snack bar/duty-free shop? ¿Dónde está la cafetería/la tienda de duty-free?
*don-de esta la ka-fe-te-**ree**-a/la **tyenda** de duty-free*

Where can I change some money? ¿Dónde puedo cambiar dinero?
*don-de **pwedo** kam**byar** dee-**ne**ro*

Where do I get the bus to town? ¿Dónde se coge el autobús para el centro?
*don-de se **ko**-khe el owto-**boos** para el **thentro***

Where are the taxis/telephones? ¿Dónde están los taxis/los teléfonos?
*don-de estan los **taksees**/los te-**le**-fonos*

I want to hire a car/reserve a hotel room Quiero alquilar un coche/reservar una habitación en un hotel
*kyero alkee-**lar** oon **ko**-che/re-ser**bar** oona abee-ta**thyon** en oon o-**tel***

I am being met Vienen a recogerme
*bye-nen a reko-**kher**-me*

airport
el aeropuerto
*a-ero-**pwerto***

baggage reclaim
la entrega de equipajes
*en-**trega** de ekee-**pa**-khes*

check-in desk
el mostrador de facturación
*mostra-**dor** de faktoo-ra**thyon***

land, to
aterrizar
*a-terre-**thar***

lounge
la sala de embarque
sala de embar-ke

non-smoking
no fumador
*no **fooma-dor***

passport control
(el control de) pasaportes
*(kon**trol** de) pasa-**por**-tes*

The Spanish alphabet is the same as the English one, with the exception of ch, ll and ñ, which are treated as separate letters. In the table below the names of the letters are shown phonetically, and each letter forms the initial of the word on the right. This is a standard system of clarification which is especially useful when spelling a word out on the telephone and in similar situations.

A	como	**Antonio**		**N**	como	**Navarra**
a	*komo*	*an-tonyo*		*e-ne*	*komo*	*na-barra*
B		**Barcelona**		**Ñ**		**Noño**
be		*bar-the-lona*		*e-nye*		*nyonyo*
C		**Carmen**		**O**		**Oviedo**
the		*karmen*		*o*		*o-byedo*
CH		**Chocolate**		**P**		**París**
che		*choko-la-te*		*pe*		*parees*
D		**Dolores**		**Q**		**Querido**
de		*dolo-res*		*koo*		*ke-reedo*
E		**Enrique**		**R**		**Ramón**
e		*enree-ke*		*e-re*		*ramon*
F		**Francia**		**S**		**Sábado**
e-fe		*franthya*		*e-se*		*sa-bado*
G		**Gerona**		**T**		**Tarragona**
khe		*khero-na*		*te*		*tarra-gona*
H		**Historia**		**U**		**Ulises**
a-che		*eesto-rya*		*oo*		*oo-lee-ses*
I		**Inés**		**V**		**Valencia**
ee		*ee-nes*		*oo-be*		*ba-lenthya*
J		**José**		**W**		**Washington**
khota		*kho-se*		*oo-be do-ble*		*wo-sheengton*
K		**Kilo**		**X**		**Xiquena**
ka		*keelo*		*e-kees*		*khee-kena*
L		**Lorenzo**		**Y**		**Yegua**
e-le		*lo-rentho*		*ee gree-e-ga*		*ye-gwa*
LL		**Llobregat**		**Z**		**Zaragoza**
e-lye		*lyo-bregat*		*theta*		*thara-gotha*
M		**Madrid**				
e-me		*madreed*				

Is it far/expensive? ¿Está lejos?/¿Es caro?
esta lekhos/es karo

Are you ...? ¿Es usted ...?
es oosted ...

Do you understand? ¿Comprende usted?
kompren-de oosted

Can I go in there? ¿Se puede entrar ahí?
se pwe-de entrar a-ee

Can you help me? ¿Me puede ayudar?
me pwe-de a-yoodar

Where is there a chemist's? ¿Dónde hay una farmacia?
don-de a-ee oona farma-thya

Where are the toilets? ¿Dónde están los servicios?
don-de estan los serbee-thyos

When will it be ready? ¿Cuándo estará listo?
kwando esta-ra leesto

How do I get there? ¿Cómo se llega ahí?
komo se lyega a-ee

How far/big is it? ¿A qué distancia está?/¿Qué tamaño tiene?
a ke deestan-thya esta/ke tama-nyo tye-ne

Is there a good restaurant? ¿Hay un buen restaurante?
a-ee oon bwen restow-ran-te

What is this? ¿Qué es esto?
ke es esto

Which is your room? ¿Cuál es su habitación?
kwal es soo abee-tathyon

Who is coming? ¿Quién va a venir?
kyen ba a beneer

How much is it? ¿Cuánto es?
kwanto es

How many kilometres? ¿Cuántos kilómetros?
kwantos keelo-metros

Is this the bus for ...? ¿Es éste el autobús de ...?
es es-te el owto-boos de ...

A red flag on a Spanish beach means that it is dangerous to go swimming. A yellow flag means that you can swim, but it is not recommended. If you see a green flag, go right ahead!

Is it safe to swim here? ¿Se puede nadar sin peligro aquí?
se pwe-de nadar seen pe-leegro a-kee

When is high/low tide? ¿A qué hora está alta/baja la marea?
a ke o-ra esta alta/bakha la ma-re-a

How deep is the water? ¿Qué profundidad tiene el agua?
ke profoon-deedad tye-ne el a-gwa

Are there strong currents? ¿Hay corrientes fuertes?
a-ee korryen-tes fwer-tes

Is it a private/quiet beach? ¿Es una playa privada/tranquila?
es oona playa pree-bada/tran-keela

Where do we change? ¿Dónde nos cambiamos?
don-de nos kam-byamos

Can I hire a deck chair/boat? ¿Puedo alquilar una tumbona/una barca?
pwedo alkee-lar oona toom-bona/oona barka

Can I go fishing/windsurfing? ¿Se puede pescar/hacer surf de vela?
se pwe-de peskar/a-ther soorf de bela

Is there a children's pool? ¿Hay una piscina para los niños?
a-ee oona pees-theena para los neenyos

Where can I get an ice-cream/ something to eat? ¿Dónde puedo comprar un helado/algo para comer?
don-de pwedo komprar oon e-lado/algo para komer

armbands	los flotadores *flota-do-res*
bucket	el cubo *koobo*
lifeguard	el vigilante *beekhee-lan-te*
sea	el mar *mar*
spade	la pala *pala*
sunglasses	las gafas de sol *gafas de sol*
sunshade	la sombrilla *sombree-lya*
suntan oil	el aceite bronceador *a-the-ee-te bron-the-a-dor*
swimsuit	el traje de baño *tra-khe de banyo*
towel	la toalla *to-a-lya*

ankle
el tobillo
tobee-lyo

arm
el brazo
bratho

back
la espalda
es-palda

body
el cuerpo
kwerpo

bone
el hueso
weso

breast
el seno/el pecho
seno/pecho

buttocks
las nalgas
nalgas

cheek
la mejilla
me-kheelya

chest
el pecho
pecho

ear
la oreja
o-rekha

elbow
el codo
kodo

eye
el ojo
o-kho

face
la cara
kara

finger
el dedo
dedo

foot
el pie
pye

hand
la mano
mano

head
la cabeza
ka-betha

heart
el corazón
kora-thon

joint
la articulación
artee-koola-thyon

kidney
el riñon
reenyon

knee
la rodilla
ro-deelya

leg
la pierna
pyerna

liver
el higado
ee-gado

lung
el pulmón
poolmon

mouth
la boca
boka

muscle
el músculo
moos-koolo

neck
el cuello
kwelyo

nose
la nariz
nareeth

shoulder
el hombro
ombro

skin
la piel
pyel

stomach
el estómago
esto-mago

throat
la garganta
gar-ganta

thumb
el pulgar
poolgar

toe
el dedo del pie
dedo del pye

tongue
la lengua
lengwa

wrist
la muñeca
moo-nyeka

See also CAR PARTS

My car has broken down Se me ha averiado el coche
se me a a-be-ryado el ko-che

There is something wrong with the brakes/electrics Los frenos no van bien/Algo falla con el sistema eléctrico
los frenos no ban byen/algo falya kon el sees-tema e-lek-treeko

I have run out of petrol Me he quedado sin gasolina
me e ke-dado seen gaso-leena

There is a leak in the radiator/petrol tank El radiador pierde agua/El depósito pierde gasolina
el radya-dor pyer-de a-gwa/el depo-seeto pyer-de gaso-leena

The engine is overheating El motor se calienta
el motor se ka-lyenta

Can you tow me to a garage? ¿Puede remolcarme hasta un garage?
pwe-de remol-kar-me asta oon gara-khe

Can you send a mechanic/a breakdown van? ¿Puede mandarme un mecánico/una grúa?
pwe-de mandar-me oon meka-neeko/oona groo-a

Do you have the parts? ¿Tiene los repuestos necesarios?
tye-ne los re-pwestos ne-the-saryos

How long will it take to repair? ¿Cuánto tardará en repararlo?
kwanto tarda-ra en repa-rarlo

Can you do a temporary repair? ¿Puede hacerle un arreglo provisional?
pwe-de ather-le oon a-rreglo probee-syonal

bulb
la bombilla
bombee-lya

emergency windscreen
el parabrisas de repuesto
para-breesas de re-pwesto

flat tyre
la rueda pinchada
rweda peen-chada

hazard lights
el intermitente de emergencia
eenter-meeten-te de emer-khenthya

jack
el gato
gato

jump leads
los cables para cargar la batería
ka-bles para kargar la ba-teree-a

spanner
la llave inglesa
lya-be een-glesa

tow rope
el cable de remolque
ka-ble de remol-ke

warning triangle
el triángulo de avería
tree-angoo-lo de a-beree-a

wheel brace
el berbiquí
berbee-kee

I have an appointment with ... Tengo una cita con ...
tengo oona theeta kon ...

He is expecting me Me está esperando
me esta es-pe-rando

Can I leave a message with his secretary? ¿Puedo dejar un
recado a su secretaria?
pwedo dekhar oon re-kado a soo se-kre-tarya

I am free tomorrow morning Estoy libre mañana por la
mañana
estoy lee-bre ma-nyana por la ma-nyana

Here is my business card Aquí tiene mi tarjeta
akee tye-ne mee tar-kheta

Can I send a telex from here? ¿Puedo mandar un télex desde
aquí?
pwedo mandar oon telex des-de akee

Where can I get some photocopying done? ¿Dónde puedo
hacer unas fotocopias?
don-de pwedo a-ther oonas foto-kopyas

I want to send this by courier Quiero enviar esto por
mensajero especial
kyero en-byar esto por mensa-khero es-pethyal

I will send you further details/a sample Le mandaré más
detalles/una muestra
le manda-re mas deta-lyes/oona mwestra

Have you a catalogue/some literature? ¿Tiene algún
catálogo/algunos folletos?
tye-ne algoon kata-logo/al-goonos fo-lyetos

I am going to the trade fair/the exhibition Voy a la feria de
muestras/a la exposición
boy a la ferya de mwestras/a la expo-seethyon

See also COLOURS AND SHAPES, DESCRIBING THINGS,
MEASUREMENTS AND QUANTITIES, PAYING, SHOPPING

Do you sell stamps? ¿Venden sellos?
 benden selyos

How much is that? ¿Cuánto es eso?
 kwanto es e-so

Have you anything smaller/bigger?
¿Tiene algo más pequeño/más grande?
 tye-ne algo mas pe-kenyo/mas gran-de

Have you got any bread/matches?
¿Tiene pan/cerillas?
 tye-ne pan/the-reelyas

I'd like a newspaper/some apples
Querría un periódico/manzanas
 kerree-a oon peryo-deeko/man-thanas

A packet of cigarettes please Un
 paquete de cigarrillos, por favor
 oon pa-ke-te de theega-reelyos, por fabor

I prefer this one Prefiero éste
 pre-fyero es-te

I'd like to see the one in the window
Querría ver el del escaparate
 kerree-a ber el del eska-para-te

I'll take this one/that one there Me
 llevo éste/ése de ahí
 me lyebo es-te/e-se de a-ee

Could you wrap it up for me please?
¿Podría envolvérmelo, por favor?
 podree-a enbol-ber-melo, por fabor

**I think you've given me the wrong
change** Me parece que se ha equivocado
 en el cambio
 *me pare-the ke se a ekee-boka-do en el
 kambyo*

100 grammes of
cien gramos de
thyen gramos de

a kilo of
un kilo de
oon keelo de

cheaper
más barato
mas ba-rato

department
el departamento
depar-tamen-to

**department
store**
los grandes
almacenes
*gran-des alma-
the-nes*

expensive
caro
karo

shop
la tienda
tyenda

supermarket
el supermercado
soo-permer-kado

Spain has many officially approved campsites; camping anywhere else is prohibited. There are four categories of campsite, and even the most basic must provide certain facilities.

We are looking for a campsite Estamos buscando un camping
es-tamos boos-kando oon kampeen

Do you have any vacancies? ¿Tienen sitio?
tye-nen seetyo

How much is it per night? ¿Cuál es la tarifa por noche?
kwal es la ta-reefa por no-che

We want to stay one night Queremos quedarnos una noche
ke-remos kedar-nos oona no-che

May we camp here? ¿Podemos acampar aquí?
po-demos akam-par a-kee

Can we park our caravan there? ¿Podemos aparcar la caravana allí?
po-demos apar-kar la kara-bana a-lyee

Is there a shop/restaurant? ¿Hay alguna tienda/algún restaurante?
a-ee algoo-na tyenda/algoon restow-ran-te

Where is the washroom/drinking water? ¿Dónde están los lavabos?/Dónde está el agua potable?
don-de estan los la-babos/don-de esta el a-gwa pota-ble

What facilities do you have on the site? ¿Qué servicios tienen en el camping?
ke ser-beethyos tye-nen en el kampeen

Is there electricity on site? ¿Hay electricidad en el camping?
a-ee elek-treethee-dad en el kampeen

air-mattress el colchón neumático
kolchon ne-ooma-teeko

camp-bed la cama de camping
kama de kampeen

fly sheet el doble techo
do-ble techo

gas cylinder la bombona de gas
bom-bona de gas

guy rope el viento
byento

mallet el mazo
matho

sleeping bag el saco de dormir
sako de dormeer

tent la tienda
tyenda

tent peg la piqueta
pee-keta (de tyenda)

tent pole el mástil
masteel

trailer el remolque
remol-ke

I want to hire a car to drive myself Quiero alquilar un coche sin conductor
kyero alkee-lar oon ko-che seen kondook-tor

I need a car with a chauffeur Necesito un coche con conductor
ne-thesee-to oon ko-che kon kondook-tor

I want a large/small car Quiero un coche grande/pequeño
kyero oon ko-che gran-de/pe-kenyo

Is there a charge per km? ¿Hay una tasa por kilómetro?
a-ee oona tasa por keelo-metro

How much extra is the comprehensive insurance cover? ¿Cuánto más cuesta el seguro a todo riesgo?
kwanto mas kwesta el segoo-ro a todo ryesgo

I would like to leave the car in ... Querría dejar el coche en ...
kerree-a dekhar el ko-che en ...

My husband/wife will be driving as well Mi marido/mujer va a conducir también
mee ma-reedo/mookher ba a kondoo-theer tambyen

Is there a radio/radio-cassette? ¿Tiene radio/radio-cassette?
tye-ne radyo/radyo-kaset

How do I operate the controls? ¿Cómo se manejan los mandos?
komo se ma-nekhan los mandos

Please explain the car documents ¿Puede explicarme los documentos del coche?
pwe-de explee-kar-me los dokoo-mentos del ko-che

accelerator
el acelerador
a-the-lera-dor

alternator
el alternador
al-terna-dor

automatic
automática
owto-matee-ka

battery
la batería
ba-teree-a

bonnet
el capó
kapo

boot
el maletero
ma-le-tero

brake fluid
el líquido de frenos
lee-keedo de frenos

brakes
los frenos
frenos

carburettor
el carburador
karboo-rador

choke
el stárter
star-ter

clutch
el embrague
embra-ge

distributor
el distribuidor
deestree-bweedor

dynamo
la dínamo
dee-namo

engine
el motor
motor

exhaust pipe
el tubo de escape
toobo de eska-pe

fan belt
la correa de
ventilador
ko-rre-a de bentee-lador

fuse
el fusible
foosee-ble

gears
las marchas
marchas

handbrake
el freno de mano
freno de mano

headlights
los faros
faros

hose
el manguito
man-geeto

ignition
el encendido
enthen-deedo

indicator
el intermitente
eenter-meeten-te

points
los platinos
pla-teenos

radiator
el radiador
radya-dor

reversing lights
las luces de marcha
atrás
loo-thes de marcha a-tras

shock absorber
el amortiguador
amor-teegwa-dor

spark plugs
las bujías
bookhee-as

steering
la dirección
deerek-thyon

steering wheel
el volante
bolan-te

tyre
el neumático
ne-oo-matee-ko

wheel
la rueda
rweda

windscreen
el parabrisas
para-breesas

windscreen washer
el lavaparabrisas
laba-para-breesas

windscreen wiper
el limpiaparabrisas
leempya-para-breesas

See also PUBLIC HOLIDAYS

When are the local festivals? ¿Cuándo son las fiestas locales?
kwando son las fyestas loka-les

Happy birthday! ¡Feliz cumpleaños!
feleeth koom-ple-a-nyos

Merry Christmas! ¡Feliz Navidad!
feleeth nabee-dad

Happy New Year! ¡Feliz Año Nuevo!
feleeth a-nyo nwebo

Congratulations! ¡Enhorabuena!
enora-bwena

Best wishes for ... Felicidades por ...
felee-theeda-des por ...

Have a good time! ¡Que se divierta!
ke se dee-byerta

Cheers! ¡Salud!
salood

Enjoy your meal! ¡Que aproveche!
ke apro-be-che

baptism
el bautismo
bow-teesmo

christening
el bautismo
bow-teesmo

holiday
las vacaciones
baka-thyo-nes

party
la fiesta
fyesta

public holiday
el día de fiesta
dee-a de fyesta

wedding
la boda
boda

**I want something for a headache/a
sore throat/toothache** Quiero algo para
el dolor de cabeza/de garganta/de muelas
*kyero algo para el dolor de ka-betha/de
gar-ganta/de mwelas*

**I would like some aspirin/sticking
plaster** Querría aspirina/tiritas
kerree-a aspee-reena/tee-reetas

**Have you anything for insect bites/
sunburn/diarrhoea?** ¿Tiene algo para
las picaduras de insectos/las quemaduras
de sol/la diarrea?
*tye-ne algo para las peeka-dooras de een-
sektos/las kema-dooras de sol/la dee-a-
rre-a*

I have a cold/a cough Tengo un
resfriado/Tengo tos
tengo oon resfree-a-do/tengo tos

**Is this suitable for an upset stomach/
hay fever?** ¿Sirve esto para un trastorno
estomacal/para la fiebre del heno?
*seer-be esto para oon tras-torno esto-
makal/para la fye-bre del e-no*

How much/how many do I take?
¿Cuánto/cuántas tomo?
kwanto/kwantas tomo

How often do I take it? ¿Cada cuánto lo
tomo?
kada kwanto lo tomo

Is it safe for children? ¿Lo pueden
tomar los niños?
lo pweden tomar los neenyos

How do I get reimbursed? ¿Cómo
consigo que me reembolsen?
komo kon-seego ke me re-embol-sen

antiseptic
el antiséptico
antee-septee-ko

bandage
la venda
benda

contraceptive
el anticonceptivo
*antee-konthep-
teebo*

cotton wool
el algodón
(hidrófilo)
*algo-don (eedro-
feelo)*

cream
la crema
krema

insect repellant
la loción contra
insectos
*lothyon kontra
een-sektos*

laxative
el laxante
laksan-te

lotion
la loción
lothyon

prescription
la receta
re-theta

sanitary towels
las compresas
kom-presas

tampons
los tampones
tampo-nes

I have two children Tengo dos niños
tengo dos neenyos

Do you have a special rate for children? ¿Tienen tarifa especial para niños?
tye-nen ta-reefa es-pethyal para neenyos

Do you have facilities for children? ¿Tienen instalaciones para niños?
tye-nen eensta-lathyo-nes para neenyos

Have you got a cot for the baby? ¿Tiene una cuna para el niño?
tye-ne oona koona para el neenyo

Do you have a special menu for children? ¿Tienen menú especial para niños?
tye-nen menoo es-pethyal para neenyos

Where can I feed/change the baby? ¿Dónde puedo dar el pecho/cambiar el pañal al niño?
don-de pwedo dar el pecho/kambyar el panyal al neenyo

Where can I warm the baby's bottle? ¿Dónde puedo calentar el biberón del niño?
don-de pwe-do kalen-tar el bee-beron del neenyo

Is there a playroom? ¿Hay alguna habitación de juegos?
a-ee algoo-na abee-tathyon de khwegos

Is there a babysitting service? ¿Hay un servicio para cuidar a los niños?
a-ee oon ser-beethyo para kweedar a los neenyos

My son is six and my daughter is nine Mi hijo tiene seis años y mi hija nueve
mee eekho tye-ne se-ees a-nyos ee mee eekha nwe-be

baby food
la comida para niños
ko-meeda para neenyos

babysitter
la cangura
kan-goora

boy
el niño
neenyo

disposable nappies
los pañales de usar y tirar
panya-les de oo-sar ee teerar

dummy
el chupete
choo-pe-te

girl
la niña
neenya

high chair
la silla alta
seelya alta

nappy
el pañal
panyal

pram
el cochecito de niño
ko-chethee-to de neenyo

push chair
la sillita de ruedas
see-lyeeta de rwedas

Where is the nearest church? ¿Dónde
queda la iglesia más próxima?
don-de keda la ee-glesya mas prok-seema

Where is there a Protestant church?
¿Dónde hay una iglesia protestante?
don-de a-ee oona ee-glesya pro-testan-te

I want to see a priest Quiero hablar con
un sacerdote
kyero a-blar kon oon sather-do-te

What time is the service? ¿A qué hora
son los oficios?
a ke ora son los o-feethyos

I want to go to confession Quiero
confesarme
kyero kon-fesar-me

altar
el altar
altar

candle
el cirio
thee-ryo

cathedral
la catedral
ka-tedral

Catholic
católico
kato-leeko

chapel
la capilla
ka-peelya

churchyard
el cementerio
themen-teryo

mass
la misa
meesa

minister
el pastor
pastor

mosque
la mezquita
meth-keeta

rabbi
el rabino
ra-beeno

synagogue
la sinagoga
seena-goga

Does this bus/train go to ...? Este
autobús/tren, ¿va a ...?
es-te owto-boos/tren ba a ...

Which number bus goes to ...? ¿Cuál es
el número del autobús que va a ...?
*kwal es el noo-mero del owto-boos ke ba
a ...*

**Where do I get a bus for the
airport/cathedral?** ¿Dónde se coge el
autobús para el aeropuerto/la catedral?
*don-de se ko-khe el owto-boos para el a-
ero-pwerto/la ka-tedral*

Which bus do I take for the museum?
¿Qué autobús cojo para ir al museo?
ke owto-boos kokho para eer al moo-se-o

Where do I change/get off? ¿Dónde
tengo que cambiar/bajarme?
don-de tengo ke kambyar/bakhar-me

**How frequent are the buses/trains to
town?** ¿Con qué frecuencia pasan los
autobuses/trenes para el centro?
*kon ke fre-kwenthya pasan los owto-boo-
ses/tre-nes para el thentro*

**Where is the nearest underground
station?** ¿Dónde queda la estación de
metro más próxima?
*don-de keda la esta-thyon de metro mas
prok-seema*

What is the fare to the town centre?
¿Cuánto vale ir al centro?
kwanto ba-le eer al thentro

Where do I buy a ticket? ¿Dónde puedo
comprar un billete?
don-de pwedo komprar oon bee-lye-te

What time is the last bus? ¿A qué hora
pasa el último autobús?
a ke o-ra pasa el ool-teemo owto-boos

book of tickets
el bonobús
bono-boos

bus stop
la parada de
autobús
*pa-rada de owto-
boos*

conductor
el cobrador
kobra-dor

driver
el conductor/la
conductora
*kondook-
tor/kondook-tora*

escalator
la escalera
mecánica
*eska-lera meka-
neeka*

half fare
el medio billete
medyo bee-lye-te

lift
el ascensor
asthen-sor

season ticket
el abono
a-bono

tourist ticket
el billete turístico
*bee-lye-te toorees-
teeko*

underground
el metro
metro

Is there a laundry service? ¿Hay servicio de lavandería?
*a-ee ser**bee**-thyo de laban-de**ree**-a*

Is there a launderette/dry cleaner's nearby? ¿Hay alguna lavandería automática/tintorería por aquí cerca?
*a-ee al-**goo**na laban-de**ree**-a owto-**matee**-ka/teento-**reree**-a por a**kee** ther**ka***

Where can I get this skirt cleaned/ironed? ¿Dónde me podrían limpiar/planchar esta falda?
*don-de me po**dree**-an leem**pyar**/plan**char** esta falda*

I need to wash this off immediately Necesito lavar esto inmediatamente
*ne-the**see**-to la**bar** esto een-medya-tamen-te*

Where can I do some washing? ¿Dónde puedo lavar?
*don-de **pwedo** la**bar***

I need soap and water Necesito agua y jabón
*ne-the**see**-to **agwa** ee kha**bon***

Where can I dry my clothes? ¿Dónde puedo poner la ropa a secar?
*don-de **pwedo** po-**ner** la **ropa** a se**kar***

This stain is coffee/blood Esta mancha es de café/sangre
*esta mancha es de ka-**fe**/sangre*

Can you remove this stain? ¿Puede quitar esta mancha?
*pwe-de kee**tar** esta mancha*

It's very delicate Es muy delicado
*es mooy delee-**kado***

When will my things be ready? ¿Para cuándo estarán mis cosas?
*para **kwando** esta-**ran** mees **kosas***

disinfectant
el desinfectante
*deseen-fek**tan**-te*

laundry room
el lavadero
*laba-**dero***

sink
el fregadero
*frega-**dero***

tap
el grifo
greefo

washbasin
el lavabo
*la-**babo***

washing powder
el jabón en polvo
*kha**bon** en **polbo***

washroom
el lavadero
*laba-**dero***

I take a continental size 40 Uso la talla
cuarenta
ooso la talya kwa-renta

Can you measure me please? ¿Puede
tomarme medida, por favor?
pwe-de tomar-me me-deeda por fabor

May I try on this dress? ¿Puedo
probarme este vestido?
pwedo probar-me es-te bes-teedo

May I take it over to the light? ¿Puedo
llevarlo a la luz?
pwedo lye-barlo a la looth

Where are the changing rooms?
¿Dónde están los probadores?
don-de estan los proba-do-res

Is there a mirror? ¿Hay algún espejo?
a-ee algoon es-pekho

It's too big/small Es demasiado grande/
pequeño
es dema-syado gran-de/pe-kenyo

What is the material? ¿Qué tejido es?
ke te-kheedo es

Is it washable? ¿Es lavable?
es laba-ble

I don't like it No me gusta
no me goosta

I don't like the colour No me gusta el
color
no me goosta el kolor

---

belt
el cinturón
theentoo-ron

blouse
la blusa
bloosa

bra
el sostèn
sos-ten

button
el botón
boton

cardigan
la rebeca
re-beka

clothes
la ropa
ropa

coat
el abrigo
a-breego

cotton
el algodón
algo-don

denim
el vaquero
ba-kero

dress
el vestido
bes-teedo

fabric
el tejido
te-kheedo

cont.

fur
las pieles
pye-les

gloves
los guantes
gwan-tes

hat
el sombrero
som-brero

jacket
la chaqueta
cha-keta

jeans
los vaqueros
ba-keros

lace
el encaje
enka-khe

leather
la piel
pyel

nightdress
el camisón
kamee-son

nylon
el nilón
neelon

panties
las bragas
bragas

pants
los calzoncillos
kalthon-theelyos

petticoat
las enaguas
e-nagwas

polyester
el polyester
polee-ester

pyjamas
el pijama
pee-khama

raincoat
el impermeable
eemper-me-a-ble

sandals
las sandalias
sanda-lyas

scarf
la bufanda
boo-fanda

shirt
la camisa
ka-meesa

shoes
los zapatos
tha-patos

shorts
los pantalones
cortos
*panta-lo-nes
kortos*

silk
la seda
seda

skirt
la falda
falda

socks
los calcetines
kal-thetee-nes

stockings
las medias
medyas

suede
el ante
an-te

suit (man's)
el traje
tra-khe

suit (woman's)
el traje
tra-khe

sweater
el suéter
swe-ter

swimsuit
el traje de baño
tra-khe de banyo

t-shirt
la camiseta
kamee-seta

tie
la corbata
kor-bata

tights
los leotardos
le-o-tardos

trousers
los pantalones
panta-lo-nes

trunks
el bañador
banya-dor

vest
la camiseta
kamee-seta

wool
la lana
lana

zip
la cremallera
krema-lyera

Is there a bus to ...? ¿Hay algún autocar para ...?
a-ee algoon owto-kar para ...

Which bus goes to ...? ¿Qué autocar va a ...?
ke owto-kar ba a ...

Where do I catch the bus for ...? ¿Dónde se coge el autocar para ...?
don-de se ko-khe el owto-kar para ...

What are the times of the buses to ...? ¿Qué horario tienen los autocares para ...?
ke o-raryo tye-nen los owto-ka-res para ...?

Does this bus go to ...? Este autocar, ¿va a ...?
es-te owto-kar ba a ...

Where do I get off? ¿Dónde tengo que bajarme?
don-de tengo ke bakhar-me

Is there a toilet on board? ¿Hay servicio en el autocar?
a-ee serbee-thyo en el owto-kar

Is there an overnight service to ...? ¿Hay un servicio nocturno para ...?
a-ee oon serbee-thyo nok-toorno para ...

What time does it leave? ¿A qué hora sale?
a ke o-ra sa-le

What time does it arrive? ¿A qué hora llega?
a ke o-ra lyega

Will you tell me where to get off? ¿Me podrá decir dónde me tengo que bajar?
me podra detheer don-de tengo ke bakhar

Let me off here Déjeme aquí
de-khe-me akee

bus depot
la estación de autocares
esta-thyon de owto-ka-res

driver
el conductor/la conductora
kondook-tor/kondook-tora

film show
la sesión de cine
sesyon de thee-ne

luggage hold
el portaequipajes
porta-ekee-pa-khes

luggage rack
la rejilla
rekhee-lya

seat
el asiento
a-syento

beige
beige
be-ees

big
grande
gran-de

black
negro
negro

blue
azul
a-thool

brown
marrón
marron

circular
circular
theerkoo-lar

crimson
carmesí
kar-mesee

cube
el cubo
koobo

dark
oscuro
oskoo-ro

fat
gordo
gordo

flat
llano
lyano

gold
dorado
do-rado

green
verde
ber-de

grey
gris
grees

lemon
color limón
kolor leemon

light
claro
klaro

long
largo
largo

mauve
malva
malba

oblong
rectangular
rektan-goolar

orange
naranja
na-rankha

oval
ovalado
oba-lado

pink
rosa
rosa

pointed
puntiagudo
poontee-a-goodo

purple
morado
mo-rado

red
rojo
rokho

round
redondo
redon-do

shade
la tonalidad
tona-leedad

shiny
brillante
breelyan-te

silver
plateado
pla-te-a-do

small
pequeño
pe-kenyo

square
cuadrado
kwa-drado

thick
grueso
grweso

thin
delgado
del-gado

tinted
matizado
matee-thado

turquoise
turquesa
toor-kesa

white
blanco
blanko

yellow
amarillo
ama-reelyo

This does not work Esto no funciona
esto no foonthyo-na

I can't turn the heating off/on No puedo apagar/encender la calefacción
*no **pwe**do apa-**gar**/enthen-**der** la ka-lefak-**thyon***

The lock is broken La cerradura está rota
*la therra-**doora** esta rota*

I can't open the window No puedo abrir la ventana
*no **pwe**do a-**breer** la ben-**tana***

The toilet won't flush No funciona la cisterna del wáter
*no foonthyo-na la thees-**terna** del **ba**-ter*

There is no hot water/toilet paper No hay agua caliente/papel higiénico
*no a-ee a-gwa ka**lyen**-te/**papel** ee-**khye**-neeko*

The washbasin is dirty El lavabo está sucio
*el la-**babo** esta **soo**thyo*

The room is noisy La habitación es ruidosa
*la abee-tathyon es rwee-**dosa***

My coffee is cold Este café está frío
*es-te ka-**fe** esta free-o*

We are still waiting to be served Todavía estamos esperando a que nos sirvan
*toda-**bee**-a es-**tamos** es-**peran**-do a ke nos **seer**ban*

I bought this here yesterday Ayer compré esto aquí
*a-**yer** kom-**pre** esto a-**kee***

It has a flaw/hole in it Tiene un defecto/agujero
*tye-ne oon de-**fek**to/agoo-**khe**ro*

How do you do? ¿Qué tal?
ke tal

Hello Hola
o-la

Goodbye Adios
a-dyos

Do you speak English? ¿Habla usted inglés?
a-bla oos-ted een-gles

I don't speak Spanish No hablo español
no a-blo espa-nyol

What's your name? ¿Cómo se llama usted?
komo se lyama oos-ted

My name is ... Me llamo ...
me lyamo ...

Do you mind if I sit here? ¿Le importa que me siente aquí?
le eem-porta ke me syen-te a-kee

I'm English/Scottish/Welsh Soy inglés/escocés/galés
soy een-gles/esko-thes/ga-les

Are you Spanish? ¿Es usted español?
es oos-ted espa-nyol

Would you like to come out with me? ¿Quiere salir conmigo?
kye-re saleer kon-meego

Yes, I should like to Si, con mucho gusto
see kon moocho goosto

No, thank you No, gracias
no grathyas

Yes please Si, por favor
  see por fabor

No thank you No, gracias
  no grathyas

Thank you (very much) (Muchas) gracias
  (*moochas*) *grathyas*

Don't mention it De nada
  de nada

I'm sorry Lo siento
  lo syento

I'm on holiday here Estoy aquí de vacaciones
  estoy a-kee de baka-thyo-nes

This is my first trip to ... Este es mi primer viaje a ...
  es-te es mee pree-mer bya-khe a ...

Do you mind if I smoke? ¿Le importa que fume?
  le eem-porta ke foo-me

Would you like a drink? ¿Quiere beber algo?
  kye-re be-ber algo

Have you ever been to England? ¿Ha estado alguna vez en
  Inglaterra?
  a es-tado al-goona beth en eengla-terra

Did you like it there? ¿Le gustó?
  le goosto

What part of Spain are you from? ¿De qué parte de España
  es usted?
  de ke par-te de espa-nya es oos-ted

In the weight and length charts, the middle figure can be either metric or imperial. Thus 3.3 feet=1 metre, 1 foot=0.3 metres, and so on.

feet		metres	inches		cm	lbs		kg
3.3	1	0.3	0.39	1	2.54	2.2	1	0.45
6.6	2	0.61	0.79	2	5.08	4.4	2	0.91
9.9	3	0.91	1.18	3	7.62	6.6	3	1.4
13.1	4	1.22	1.57	4	10.6	8.8	4	1.8
16.4	5	1.52	1.97	5	12.7	11	5	2.2
19.7	6	1.83	2.36	6	15.2	13.2	6	2.7
23	7	2.13	2.76	7	17.8	15.4	7	3.2
26.2	8	2.44	3.15	8	20.3	17.6	8	3.6
29.5	9	2.74	3.54	9	22.9	19.8	9	4.1
32.9	10	3.05	3.9	10	25.4	22	10	4.5
			4.3	11	27.9			
			4.7	12	30.1			

°C	0	5	10	15	17	20	22	24	26	28	30	35	37	38	40	50	100
°F	32	41	50	59	63	68	72	75	79	82	86	95	98.4	100	104	122	212

Km	10	20	30	40	50	60	70	80	90	100	110	120
Miles	6.2	12.4	18.6	24.9	31	37.3	43.5	49.7	56	62	68.3	74.6

Tyre pressures

lb/sq in	15	18	20	22	24	26	28	30	33	35
kg/sq cm	1.1	1.3	1.4	1.5	1.7	1.8	2	2.1	2.3	2.5

Liquids

gallons	1.1	2.2	3.3	4.4	5.5	pints	0.44	0.88	1.76
litres	5	10	15	20	25	litres	0.25	0.5	1

I have nothing to declare No tengo nada que declarar
*no **tengo nada** que dekla-**rar***

I have the usual allowances of alcohol/tobacco Llevo la
cantidad permitida de alcohol/tabaco
*lyebo la kantee-**dad** permee-**teeda** de al**kol**/ta-**bako***

I have two bottles of wine/a bottle of spirits to declare
Tengo dos botellas de vino/una botella de licor que declarar
*tengo dos bo-**telyas** de **beeno**/oona bo-**telya** de lee**kor** ke dekla-
rar*

My wife/husband and I have a joint passport Mi
mujer/marido y yo tenemos un pasaporte familiar
*mee moo-**kher**/ma-**reedo** ee yo te-**nemos** oon pasa-**por**-te
famee-**lyar***

The children are on this passport Los niños están en este
pasaporte
*los **neenyos** estan en **es**-te pasa-**por**-te*

I am a British national Soy súbdito británico
*soy **soob**-deeto breeta-**neeko***

I shall be staying in this country for three weeks Voy a
pasar tres semanas en este país
*boy a pa**sar** tres se-**manas** en **es**-te pa-**ees***

We are here on holiday Venimos de vacaciones
*be-**neemos** de baka-**thyo**-nes*

I am here on business He venido de negocios
*e be-**needo** de ne-**gothyos***

I have an entry visa Tengo un visado (de entrada)
*tengo oon bee-**sado** (de en-**trada**)*

See also NUMBERS

What is the date today? ¿Qué fecha es hoy?
kay fecha es oy

It's the ...   Es el ...   *es el ...*
1st of March	2nd of June
primero de marzo	dos de junio
pree-mero de martho	*dos de khoonyo*

We will arrive on the 29th of August
Llegaremos el veintinueve de agosto
lyega-remos el be-een-tee-nwe-be de a-gosto

1984 mil novecientos ochenta y cuatro
meel no-be-thyentos o-chenta ee kwatro

Monday	lunes	*loo-nes*
Tuesday	martes	*mar-tes*
Wednesday	miércoles	*myerko-les*
Thursday	jueves	*khwe-bes*
Friday	viernes	*byer-nes*
Saturday	sábado	*sa-bado*
Sunday	domingo	*domeen-go*

January	May	September
enero	mayo	septiembre
e-nero	*mayo*	*sep-tyembre*
February	**June**	**October**
febrero	junio	octubre
fe-brero	*khoonyo*	*oktoo-bre*
March	**July**	**November**
marzo	julio	noviembre
martho	*khoolyo*	*nobyem-bre*
April	**August**	**December**
abril	agosto	diciembre
a-breel	*a-gosto*	*deethyem-bre*

You will be asked to pay for treatment on the spot, so medical insurance is essential.

I need to see the dentist (urgently) Necesito ver (urgentemente) al dentista
*ne-the**see**-to ber (oor-khen-te**men**-te) al den-**tees**ta*

I have toothache Me duele una muela
*me **dwe**-le oona **mwe**la*

I've broken a tooth Me he roto un diente
*me e **ro**to oon **dyen**-te*

A filling has come out Se me ha caido un empaste
*se me a ka-**ee**do oon em**pas**-te*

My gums are bleeding/are sore Me sangran/me duelen las encias
*me **sangran**/me **dwe**-len las en**thee**-as*

Please give me an injection Póngame una inyección, por favor
*ponga-me oona een-yek**thyon** por fa**bor***

My dentures need repairing Necesito que me arregle la dentadura postiza
*ne-the**see**-to ke me a-**rre**-gle la denta-**doo**ra pos-**tee**tha*

THE DENTIST MAY SAY:

Tendré que sacársela
*ten-**dre** ke sa**kar**-sela*
I shall have to take it out

Necesita un empaste
*ne-the-**see**ta oon em**pas**-te*
You need a filling

Esto puede que le duela un poco
*esto pwe-de ke le **dwe**-le oon **po**ko*
This might hurt a bit

bad
malo
malo

beautiful
hermoso
er-moso

bitter
amargo
a-margo

clean
limpio
leempyo

cold
frio
free-o

difficult
dificil
dee-feetheel

dirty
sucio
soothyo

easy
fácil
fatheel

excellent
excelente
ex-thelen-te

far
lejos
lekhos

fast
rápido
ra-peedo

good
bueno
bweno

hard
duro
dooro

heavy
pesado
pe-sado

horrible
horrible
o-rree-ble

hot
caliente
kalyen-te

interesting
interesante
een-te-resan-te

light
ligero
lee-khero

long
largo
largo

lovely
bonito
bo-neeto

near
cerca
therka

new
nuevo
nwebo

old
aburrido
aboo-rreedo

pleasant
agradable
agra-da-ble

rough
áspero
a-spero

short
corto
korto

slow
lento
lento

smooth
suave
swa-be

soft
blando
blando

sour
agrio
a-gree-o

spicy
picante
peekan-te

strong
fuerte
fwer-te

sweet
dulce
dool-the

unpleasant
desagradable
des-agra-da-ble

warm
cálido
ka-leedo

weak
débil/flojo
debeel/flokho

Where is the nearest post office?
¿Dónde queda la oficina de correos más
próxima?
*don-de keda la ofee-theena de ko-rre-os
mas prok-seema*

How do I get to the airport? ¿Cómo se
va al aeropuerto?
komo se ba al a-e-ropwer-to

Is this the right way to the cathedral?
¿Se va por aquí a la catedral?
se ba por a-kee a la ka-tedral

**I am looking for the tourist
information office** Busco la oficina de
turismo
boosko la ofee-theena de too-reesmo

Is it far to walk/by car? ¿Queda lejos
para ir andando/para ir en coche?
*keda lekhos para eer andan-do/para eer en
ko-che*

Which road do I take for ...? ¿Cuál es la
carretera de ...?
kwal es la ka-rre-tera de ...

Is this the turning for ...? ¿Se va por
aqui a ...?
se ba por a-kee a ...

How do I get on to the motorway? ¿Por
dónde he de ir para coger la autopista?
*por don-de e de eer para ko-kher la owto-
peesta*

I have lost my way Me he perdido
me e per-deedo

Can you show me on the map? ¿Puede
indicármelo en el mapa?
pwe-de eendee-kar-melo en el mapa

How long will it take to get there?
¿Cuánto se tarda en llegar?
kwanto se tarda en lyegar

---

corner
la esquina
es-keena

left
(a la) izquierda
(a la) eeth-kyerda

near
cerca
therka

over
por encima de
por en-theema de

over there
alli
a-lyee

right
(a la) derecha
(a la) de-recha

road sign
la señal de tráfico
senyal de tra-feeko

station
la estación
esta-thyon

straight on
todo recto
todo rekto

through
por
por

under
debajo de
de-bakho de

See also BODY
If you visit the doctor you will have to pay on the spot, so make sure you are properly insured before you leave.

I need a doctor Necesito un médico
ne-thesee-to oon me-deeko

Can I have an appointment with the doctor? ¿Puede darme hora para el médico?
pwe-de dar-me o-ra para el me-deeko

My son/wife is ill Mi hijo está enfermo/ Mi mujer está enferma
mee ee-kho esta enfer-mo/mee mookher esta enfer-ma

I have a sore throat/a stomach upset Me duele la garganta/Tengo un trastorno estomacal
me dwe-le la gar-ganta/tengo oon trastorno esto-makal

He has diarrhoea/earache Tiene diarrea/dolor de oídos
tye-ne dee-a-rre-a/dolor de o-eedos

I am constipated Tengo estreñimiento
tengo es-tre-nyee-myento

I have a pain in my chest/here Tengo un dolor en el pecho/aquí
tengo oon dolor en el pecho/a-kee

She has a temperature Tiene fiebre
tye-ne fye-bre

He has been stung by a wasp/bitten by a dog Le ha picado una avispa/Le ha mordido un perro
le a pee-kado oona a-beespa/le a mor-deedo oon perro

He can't breathe/walk No puede respirar/andar
no pwe-de respee-rar/andar

cough
la tos
tos

cut
el corte
kor-te

faint, to
desmayarse
desma-yar-se

food poisoning
la intoxicación por alimentos
eentok-seeka-thyon por alee-mentos

hay fever
la fiebre del heno
fye-bre del e-no

headache
el dolor de cabeza
dolor de ka-betha

I feel dizzy Me siento mareado
*me **syent**o ma-re-a-do*

I can't sleep/swallow No puedo
dormir/respirar
*no **pwed**o dor**meer**/respee-**rar***

She has been sick Ha vomitado
*a bomee-**ta**do*

I am a diabetic/pregnant Soy
diabético/Estoy embarazada
*soy dee-a-**bete**-ko/**estoy** emba-ratha-da*

I am allergic to penicillin/cortisone
Soy alérgico a la penicilina/cortisona
*soy a-**lerk**hee-ko a la penee-thee**lee**-na/kortee-**so**na*

I have high blood pressure Tengo la
tensión alta
*tengo la ten**syon** alta*

**My blood group is A positive/O
negative** Mi grupo sanguíneo es A
positivo/cero negativo
*mee **groo**po san**gee**-ne-o es a posee-**teeb**o/**thero** nega-**teeb**o*

THE DOCTOR MAY SAY:

Tiene que quedarse en la cama
*tye-ne ke ke**dar**-se en la **ka**ma*
You must stay in bed

Tendrá que ir al hospital
*ten**dra** ke eer al ospee-**tal***
He will have to go to hospital

Va a necesitar una operación
*ba a ne-thesee-**tar** oona o-pera-**thyon***
You will need an operation

Tómese esto tres/cuatro veces al día
*to-me-se esto tres/**kwa**tro be-thes al **dee**-a*
Take this three/four times a day

inflamed inflamado *eenfla-**mado***	
injection la inyección *eenyek-**thyon***	
medicine la medicina *medee-**thee**na*	
painful doloroso *dolo-**roso***	
pill la píldora ***peel**-dora*	
poisoning el envenenamiento *en-be-nena-**myento***	
tablet la pastilla *pas-**teel**ya*	
unconscious inconsciente *eenkons-**thyen**-te*	

See also WINES AND SPIRITS

A black/white coffee, please Un café
solo/un café con leche, por favor
*oon ka-fe solo/oon ka-fe kon le-che por
fabor*

Two cups of tea Dos tes
dos tes

A pot of tea for four Té para cuatro
te para kwa-tro

A glass of lemonade Una limonada
oona leemo-nada

A bottle of mineral water Una botella
de agua mineral
oona bo-telya de a-gwa mee-neral

A draught beer Una caña
oona kanya

Do you have ...? ¿Tienen ...?
tye-nen...

With ice, please Con hielo, por favor
kon yelo por fabor

Another coffee, please Otro café, por
favor
o-tro ka-fe por fabor

beer
la cerveza
ther-betha

coke
la coca cola
koka kola

drinking chocolate
el chocolate
(deshecho)
choko-la-te (des-e-cho)

drinking water
el agua potable
a-gwa pota-ble

fruit juice
el zumo
thoomo

lemon tea
el té con limón
te kon leemon

milk
la leche
le-che

shandy
la cerveza con
limonada
*ther-betha kon
leemo-nada*

soft drink
la bebida no
alcohólica
*be-beeda no alko-
leeka*

with milk
con leche
kon le-che

See also ACCIDENTS - CARS, BREAKDOWNS, CAR PARTS, PETROL STATION, POLICE, ROAD SIGNS

Speed limits are 60 km/h in towns, 90 km/h on ordinary roads, and 100 on motorways.

What is the speed limit on this road?
¿Qué límite de velocidad hay en esta carretera?
*ke **lee**mee-te de belo-thee**dad** a-ee en esta ka-rre-**tera***

Are seat belts compulsory? ¿Es obligatorio el uso del cinturón de seguridad?
*es oblee-**gato**-ryo el **oo**-so del theentoo-**ron** de segoo-reedad*

Is there a toll on this motorway? ¿Es de peaje esta autopista?
*es de pe-a-khe esta owto-**peesta***

What is causing this hold-up? ¿A qué se debe este atasco?
*a ke se **de**-be es-te a-**tasko***

Is there a short cut? ¿Hay algún atajo?
*a-ee al**goon** a-**takho***

Where can I park? ¿Dónde puedo aparcar?
*don-de pwedo apar-**kar***

Is there a car park nearby? ¿Hay algún aparcamiento por aquí cerca?
*a-ee al**goon** apar-kamyen-to por a-**kee** therka*

Can I park here? ¿Se puede aparcar aquí?
*se pwe-de apar-**kar** a-**kee***

How long can I stay here? ¿Cuánto tiempo puedo quedarme aquí?
*kwanto tyempo pwedo kedar-me a-**kee***

Do I need a parking disc? ¿Hace falta disco de estacionamiento?
*a-the **falta deesko** de esta-thyona-**myento***

driving licence	el permiso de conducir *per-**meeso** de kondoo-**theer***
green card	la carta verde *karta ber-de*
major road	la carretera *ka-rre-**tera***
minor road	la carretera secundaria *ka-rre-**tera** sekoon-darya*
one-way	de dirección única *de deerek-**thyon** oo-neeka*
parking meter	el parquímetro *parkee-metro*
parking ticket	la multa por aparcamiento indebido ***moolta** por apar-kamyen-to eende-beedo*
sign	la señal *senyal*
traffic lights	el semáforo *sema-foro*

See also DRINKS, FOOD, ORDERING, PAYING
Spanish restaurants are graded with one to five forks, and you
can have memorable meals whether you eat in elegant
restaurants or local inns. Set-price menus are usually good value,
but avoid *menús turísticos* in places which obviously cater for
tourists.

Is there a restaurant/café near here?
¿Hay algún restaurante/alguna cafetería
por aquí cerca?
*a-ee al**goon** restow-**ran**-te/al**goo**-na ka-fe-
teree-a por a-**kee ther**ka*

A table for four Una mesa para cuatro
*oona **mesa** para **kwa**tro*

May we see the menu? ¿Nos trae la
carta?
*nos tra-e la **karta***

We'll take the set menu please
Tráiganos el plato del día, por favor
*tra-eega-nos el **plato** del **dee**-a por fa**bor***

We'd like a drink first Querríamos beber
algo primero
*kerree-amos be**ber** algo pree-**mero***

Do you have a menu for children?
¿Tienen un menú especial para los niños?
*tye-nen oon me**noo** es-pe**thyal** para los
neenyos*

**Could we have some more bread/
water?** ¿Nos trae más pan/agua?
nos tra-e mas pan/a-gwa

**We'd like a dessert/some mineral
water** Queremos postre/agua mineral
*ke-**remos** **pos**-tre/a-gwa mee-ne**ral***

The bill, please La cuenta, por favor
*la **kwenta** por fa**bor***

Is service included? ¿Va incluido el
servicio?
*ba eenkloo-**eedo** el ser-**beethyo***

cheese
el queso
keso

main course
el plato principal
*plato preenthee-
pal*

sandwich
el bocadillo
*boka-**deel**yo*

soup
la sopa
sopa

starter
el entremés
*en-tre-**mes***

terrace
la terraza
*te-**rratha***

vegetables
las verduras
berdoo-ras

See also ACCIDENTS, BREAKDOWNS, DENTIST, DOCTOR

There's a fire! ¡Hay fuego!
a-ee fwego

Call a doctor/an ambulance! ¡Llame a
un médico/a una ambulancia!
lya-me a oon me-deeko/a oona amboo-lanthya

We must get him to hospital Tenemos
que llevarlo al hospital
te-nemos ke lyebar-lo al ospee-tal

Fetch help quickly Vaya a buscar ayuda,
¡de prisa!
baya a booskar a-yooda de preesa

He can't swim No sabe nadar
no sa-be nadar

Get the police Llame a la policía
lya-me a la polee-thee-a

**Where's the nearest police station/
hospital?** ¿Dónde queda la comisaría
más próxima/el hospital más próximo?
don-de keda la komee-saree-a mas prok-seema/el ospee-tal mas prok-seemo

I've lost my credit card/wallet He
perdido la tarjeta de crédito/la cartera
he per-deedo la tar-kheta de kre-deeto/la kar-tera

My child/handbag is missing Se me ha
perdido mi hijo/el bolso
se me a per-deedo mee eekho/el bolso

My passport/watch has been stolen Me
han robado el pasaporte/el reloj
me an ro-bado el pasa-por-te/el relo

I've forgotten my ticket/my key Se me
ha olvidado el billete/la llave
se me a olbee-dado el bee-lye-te/la lya-be

coastguard
el guardacostas
gwarda-kostas

consulate
el consulado
konsoo-lado

embassy
la embajada
emba-khada

fire brigade
los bomberos
bom-beros

fire!
¡fuego!
fwego

help!
¡socorro!
so-korro

**lost property
office**
la oficina de
objetos perdidos
ofee-theena de ob-khetos per-deedos

police!
¡policía!
polee-thee-a

stop thief!
¡al ladrón!
al ladron

See also NIGHTLIFE, SIGHTSEEING

Are there any local festivals? ¿Hay
fiestas locales?
a-ee fyestas loka-les

**Can you recommend something for
the children?** ¿Puede recomendar algo
para los niños?
*pwe-de reko-mendar algo para los
neenyos*

What is there to do in the evenings?
¿Qué se puede hacer por las noches?
ke se pwe-de a-ther por las no-ches

Where is there a cinema/theatre?
¿Dónde hay un cine/un teatro?
don-de a-ee oon thee-ne/oon te-a-tro

Where can we go to a concert? ¿Dónde
podemos asistir a algún concierto?
*don-de po-demos asees-teer a algoon
kon-thyerto*

Can you book the tickets for us?
¿Puede sacarnos las entradas usted?
pwe-de sakar-nos las en-tradas oos-ted

Are there any night clubs/discos?
¿Hay algún nightclub/alguna discoteca?
*a-ee algoon nightkloob/algoo-na deesko-
teka*

Is there a swimming pool? ¿Hay
piscina?
a-ee pees-theena

Can we go riding/fishing? ¿Se puede
montar a caballo/pescar?
se pwe-de montar a ka-balyo/peskar

Where can we play tennis/golf?
¿Dónde se puede jugar al tenis/al golf?
*don-de se pwe-de khoogar al tenees/al
golf*

**admission
charge**
el precio de
entrada
*prethyo de en-
trada*

bar
el bar
bar

booking office
el despacho de
billetes
*des-pacho de bee-
lye-tes*

club
el club
kloob

fun fair
el parque de
atracciones
*par-ke de atrak-
thyo-nes*

jazz
el jazz
yas

orchestra
la orquesta
or-kesta

play
la obra de teatro
o-bra de te-a-tro

show
el espectáculo
espek-takoo-lo

ticket
el billete
bee-lye-te

What time is the next sailing? ¿A qué hora sale el próximo (ferry)?
a ke o-ra sa-le el prok-seemo (ferry)

A return ticket for one car, two adults and two children Un billete de ida y vuelta para un coche con dos adultos y dos niños
oon bee-lye-te de eeda ee bwelta para oon ko-che kon dos a-dooltos ee dos neenyos

How long does the crossing take? ¿Cuánto dura la travesía?
kwanto doora la tra-besee-a

Are there any cabins/reclining seats? ¿Hay camarotes/sillones recostables?
a-ee kama-ro-tes/seelyo-nes rekos-ta-bles

Is there a bar/TV lounge? ¿Hay bar/sala de television?
a-ee bar/sala de te-lebee-syon

Where are the toilets? ¿Dónde están los servicios?
don-de estan los ser-beethyos

Where is the duty-free shop? ¿Dónde está la tienda de duty-free?
don-de esta la tyenda de duty-free

Can we go out on deck? ¿Podemos salir a la cubierta?
po-demos saleer a la koo-byerta

What is the sea like today? ¿Cómo está hoy el mar?
komo esta oy el mar

---

captain
el capitán
kapee-tan

crew
la tripulación
treepoo-lathyon

hovercraft
el aerodeslizador
a-ero-deslee-thador

life jacket
el chaleco salvavidas
cha-leko salba-beedas

lifeboat
el bote salvavidas
bo-te salba-beedas

purser
el contador de navio
konta-dor de nabee-o

rough
agitado
akhee-tado

ship
el barco
barko

smooth
calmado
kal-mado

the Channel
el Canal de la Mancha
kanal de la mancha

beef
la carne de vaca
kar-ne de *ba*ka

bread
el pan
pan

butter
la mantequilla
man-te*kee*-lya

cheese
el queso
keso

chicken
el pollo
polyo

coffee
el café
ka-*fe*

cream
la nata
nata

eggs
los huevos
webos

fish
el pescado
pes-*kado*

flour
la harina
a-*reena*

ham
el jamón
khamon

jam
la mermelada
mer-mela-*da*

kidneys
los riñones
reenyo-*nes*

kilo
el kilo
keelo

lamb
el cordero
kor-*dero*

litre
el litro
leetro

liver
el hígado
ee-gado

margarine
la margarina
marga-*reena*

milk
la leche
le-che

mince
la carne picada
kar-ne pee-*kada*

mustard
la mostaza
mos-*tatha*

oil
el aceite
a-*the*-ee-te

pepper
la pimienta
pee-*myenta*

pork
el cerdo
therdo

pound
la libra
leebra

rice
el arroz
a-*rroth*

salt
la sal
sal

soup
la sopa
sopa

steak
el filete
fee-*le*-te

sugar
el azúcar
a-*thookar*

tea
el té
te

tin
la lata
lata

veal
la ternera
ter-*nera*

vinegar
el vinagre
beena-*gre*

yoghurt
el yogur
yo*goor*

apples
las manzanas
man-thanas

asparagus
los espárragos
espa-rragos

aubergine
la berenjena
beren-khena

avocado
el aguacate
agwa-ka-te

bananas
los plátanos
pla-tanos

beetroot
la remolacha
remo-lacha

carrots
las zanahorias
thana-o-ryas

cauliflower
la coliflor
kolee-flor

celery
el apio
a-pyo

cherries
las cerezas
the-rethas

courgettes
los calabacines
kala-bathee-nes

cucumber
el pepino
pe-peeno

french beans
las judías verdes
khoodee-as ber-des

garlic
el ajo
a-kho

grapefruit
el pomelo
po-melo

grapes
las uvas
oo-bas

leeks
los puerros
pwerros

lemon
el limón
leemon

lettuce
la lechuga
le-chooga

melon
el melón
melon

mushrooms
los champiñones
champee-nyo-nes

olives
las aceitunas
a-the-ee-toonas

onions
las cebollas
the-bolyas

oranges
las naranjas
na-rankhas

peaches
los melocotones
melo-koto-nes

pears
las peras
peras

peas
los guisantes
geesan-tes

pepper
el pimiento
verde/rojo
pee-myento ber-de/rokho

pineapple
la piña
peenya

plums
las ciruelas
thee-rwelas

potatoes
las patatas
pa-tatas

radishes
los rábanos
ra-banos

raspberries
las frambuesas
fram-bwesas

spinach
las espinacas
espee-nakas

strawberries
las fresas
fresas

tomatoes
los tomates
toma-tes

Where can we buy souvenirs of the cathedral? ¿Dónde podemos comprar recuerdos de la catedral?
don-de po-demos komprar re-kwerdos de la ka-tedral

Where is the nearest gift shop? ¿Dónde queda la tienda de regalos más próxima?
don-de keda la tyenda de re-galos mas prok-seema

I want to buy a present for my husband/wife Quiero comprar un regalo para mi marido/mi mujer
kyero komprar oon re-galo para mee ma-reedo/moo-kher

What is the local/regional speciality? ¿Qué es lo típico de aquí/de la zona?
ke es lo tee-peeko de a-kee/de la tho-na

Is this hand-made? ¿Es esto hecho a mano?
es esto e-cho a mano

Have you anything suitable for a young child? ¿Tienen alguna cosa para un niño pequeño?
tye-nen al-goona kosa para oon neenyo pe-kenyo

I want something cheaper/more expensive Querría algo más barato/más caro
kerree-a algo mas ba-rato/mas karo

Will this cheese/wine travel well? ¿Aguantará bien el viaje este queso/vino?
agwan-tara byen el bya-khe es-te keso/beeno

Please wrap it up for me Haga el favor de envolvérmelo
a-ga el fabor de enbol-ber-melo

bracelet
la pulsera
pool-sera

brooch
el broche
bro-che

chocolates
los chocolates
choko-la-tes

earrings
los pendientes
pendyen-tes

flowers
las flores
flo-res

necklace
el collar
kolyar

ornament
el ornamento
orna-mento

perfume
el perfume
perfoo-me

pottery
la cerámica
thera-meeka

ring
el anillo
a-neelyo

table linen
la mantelería
man-te-leree-a

watch
el reloj
relo

Nouns

Spanish nouns are *masculine* or *feminine*, and their gender is shown by the words for 'the' and 'a' used before them (the 'article'):

MASCULINE	FEMININE
el/un castillo *the/a castle*	**la/una** mesa *the/a table*
los castillos/**(unos)** castillos	**las** mesas/**(unas)** mesas
the castles/castles	*the tables/tables*

It is usually possible to tell whether a noun is masculine or feminine by its ending: nouns ending on **-o** or **-or** are generally masculine, while those ending in **-a, -dad, -ión, -tud** and **-umbre** tend to be feminine. There are exceptions, however, and it's best to learn the noun and the article together. (Note that feminine nouns which begin with a stressed **a-** or **ha-** take the masculine singular definite article, *el*).

Plural

Nouns ending in a vowel form the plural by adding **-s,** while those ending in a consonant or a stressed vowel add **-es.** The **-z** ending changes to **-ces** in the plural: *la voz, las voces.*
NOTE: When used after the words **a** (to) and **de** (of, from), **el** contracts as follows:

> **a + el → al** *al*
> **de + el → del** *del*
> e.g. **al** cine (*to the cinema*)
> el precio **del** billete (*the price of the ticket*)

'This', 'That', 'These', 'Those'

These depend on the gender and number of the noun they represent:

este niño	*this boy*	**esta** niña	*this girl*
estos niños	*these boys*	**estas** niñas	*these girls*
ese niño	*that boy*	**esa** niña	*that girl*
esos niños	*those boys*	**esas** niñas	*those girls*
aquel niño	*that boy*	**aquella** niña	*that girl*
	(over there)		*(over there)*
aquellos niños	*those boys*	**aquellas** niñas	*those girls*
	(over there)		*(over there)*

Adjectives

Adjectives normally follow the noun noun they describe in Spanish, e.g. la manzana roja (the red apple). Some common exceptions which *precede* the noun are:

> **mucho** much, many; **poco** few; **tanto** so much, so many; **primero** first; **último** last; **bueno** good; **malo** bad; **ninguno** no, not any; **grande** great.

Spanish adjectives have to reflect the gender of the noun they describe. To make an adjective *feminine*, **-o** endings change to **-a**, and **-án**, **-ón**, **-or** and **-és** change to **-ana**, **-ona**, **-ora** and **-esa**. Other adjectives have the the same form for both genders. Thus:

MASCULINE	el libro **rojo**	FEMININE	la manzana **roja**
	(the red book)		(the red apple)
	el hombre **hablador**		la mujer **habladora**
	(the talkative man)		(the talkative woman)

To make an adjective plural **-s** is added to the singular form if it ends in a vowel, **-es** if it ends in a consonant:

los libros **rojos**	los libros **útiles**
(the red books)	(the useful books)

'My', 'Your', 'His', 'Her'

These words also depend on the gender and number of the following noun and not on the sex of the 'owner'.

	with masculine	with feminine	with plural nouns
my	**mi** (*mee*)	**mi** (*mee*)	**mis** (*mees*)
his/her/			
its/your	**su** (*soo*)	**su** (*soo*)	**sus** (*soos*)
our	**nuestro** (*nwestro*)	**nuestra** (*nwestra*)	**nuestros/nuestras** (*nwestros/nwestras*)
their/your	**su** (*soo*)	**su** (*soo*)	**sus** (*soos*)

NOTE: There is no distinction between 'his' and 'her':

> **el** billete → **su** billete (whether the owner is 'he' or 'she').

Pronouns

SUBJECT		OBJECT	
I	**yo** (*yo*)	me	**me** (*me*)
you	**usted** (*oos-ted*)	you	**le** (*le*)
he	**él** (*el*)	him	**le, lo** (*le, lo*)
she	**ella** (*e-lya*)	her	**le, la** (*le, la*)
it	**él/ella** (*el/e-lya*)	it	**lo, la** (*lo,la*)
we	**nosotros** (*nos-otros*)	us	**nos** (*nos*)
you	**ustedes** (*oos-te-des*)	you	**les** (*les*)
they	(masc) **ellos** (*e-lyos*)	them (masc)	**les, los** (*les, los*)
	(fem) **ellas** (*e-lyas*)	(fem)	**les, las** (*les, las*)

NOTES

1. Subject pronouns are normally not used except for emphasis or to avoid confusion:

> **yo** voy a Mallorca y **él** va a Alicante

2. Object pronouns are placed before the verb:

> **le** veo *le be-o*
> I see him/her
> **le** conocemos *le kono-themos*
> we know him/her

However, in commands or requests, the pronouns follow the verb, as in English:

> ayúde**me** *a-yoo-de-me*
> help me
> escúche**le** *eskoo-che-le*
> listen to him

BUT in commands expressed in the negative, e.g. don't do it, the pronouns *precede* the verb.

3. The object pronouns shown above can be used to mean *to me*, *to us*, etc, except that **lo** becomes **le**:

> **me** da el libro *me da el leebro*
> he gives me the book

However, if **le/les** occur in combinations with **lo/la/los/las**, then **le/les** changes to **se**:

> **se** lo doy *se lo doy*
> I give it to him/her/you

4. The pronoun following a preposition has the same form as the subject pronoun, except for **mi** (*mee*) me and **ti** (*tee*) you.

Verbs

There are three main patterns of endings for verbs in Spanish-those ending in **-ar**, **-er** and **-ir** in the dictionary.

cantar to sing	**temer** to fear	**partir** to leave
canto I sing	**temo** I fear	**parto** I leave
canta he/she/it sings/you sing	**teme** he/she/it fears/you fear	**parte** he/she/it leaves/you leave
cantamos we sing	**tememos** we fear	**partimos** we leave
cantan they/you sing	**temen** they/you fear	**parten** they/you leave

And in the past tense:

he cantado I sang	**he temido** I feared	**he partido** I left
ha cantado he/she/ it/you sang	**ha temido** he/she/ it/you feared	**ha partido** he/she/ it/you left
hemos cantado we sang	**hemos temido** we feared	**hemos partido** we left
han cantado they/ you sang	**han temido** they/ you feared	**han partido** they/ you left

Four of the most common verbs are irregular:

ser to be	**estar** to be
soy I am	**estoy** I am
es he/she/it is/you are	**está** he/she/it is/you are
somos we are	**estamos** we are
son they/you are	**estan** they/you are
tener to have	**ir** to go
tengo I have	**voy** I go
tiene he/she/it has/you have	**va** he/she/it goes/you go
tenemos we have	**vamos** we go
tienen they/you have	**van** they/you go

Spanish has two forms of address, formal and informal. You should only use the informal *tú* when talking to someone you know well; the normal word for "you" is *usted*. Spaniards also use the words *señor*, *señora* and *señorita* a great deal, and shake hands on meeting and on saying goodbye.

Hello Hola
 o-la

Good morning/good afternoon Buenos días
 bwenos dee-as

Good afternoon/good evening Buenas tardes
 bwenas tar-des

Good evening/good night Buenas noches
 bwenas no-ches

Goodbye Adiós
 a-dyos

How do you do? ¿Qué tal?
 ke tal

Pleased to meet you Mucho gusto
 moocho goosto

How nice to see you Me alegro de verle
 me a-legro de ber-le

How are you? ¿Cómo está usted?
 komo esta oos-ted

Fine thank you Bien, gracias
 byen grathyas

See you soon Hasta pronto
 asta pronto

See you later Hasta luego
 asta lwego

I'd like to make an appointment
Querría pedir hora
ke-rree-a pedeer o-ra

A cut and blow-dry please Corte y
secado a mano, por favor
kor-te ee se-kado a mano por fabor

A shampoo and set Lavado y marcado
la-bado ee mar-kado

Not too short No me lo corte demasiado
no me lo kor-te dema-syado

I'd like it layered Lo quiero en capas
lo kyero en kapas

Not too much off the back/the fringe
No me lo corte demasiado por detrás/por
delante
*no me lo kor-te dema-syado por detras/
por delan-te*

Take more off the top/the sides
Córtemelo más por arriba/por los lados
kor-te-melo mas por a-rreeba/por los lados

My hair is permed/tinted Tengo
permanente/el pelo teñido
tengo perma-nen-te/el pelo te-nyeedo

My hair is naturally curly/straight
Tengo el pelo rizado/liso
tengo el pelo ree-thado/leeso

It's too hot Está demasiado caliente
esta dema-syado kalyen-te

I'd like a conditioner please ¿Me pone
crema suavizante, por favor?
me po-ne crema swabee-than-te por fabor

I'd like some hair spray ¿Me pone laca?
me po-ne laka

gown	el traje
	tra-khe
haircut	el corte
	kor-te
long	largo
	largo
parting	la raya
	raya
perm	la permanente
	perma-nen-te
shampoo	el champú
	champoo
short	corto
	korto
streaks	las mechas
	mechas
styling mousse	el fijador
	feekha-dor
towel	la toalla
	to-a-lya
trim	el recorte
	rekor-te

See also ACCOMMODATION, ROOM SERVICE, PAYING

I have reserved a room in the name of ... Tengo reservada una habitación a nombre de ...
tengo reser-bada oona abee-tathyon a nom-bre de ...

I confirmed my booking by phone/by letter Confirmé la reserva por teléfono/por carta
konfeer-me la re-serba por te-le-fono/por karta

Could you have my luggage taken up? ¿Puede mandar que me suban el equipaje?
pwe-de mandar ke me sooban el ekee-pa-khe

What time is breakfast/dinner? ¿A qué hora es el desayuno/la cena?
a ke o-ra es el desa-yoono/la thena

Can we have breakfast in our room? ¿Pueden traernos el desayuno a la habitación?
pwe-den tra-ernos el desa-yoono a la abee-tathyon

Call me at seven thirty Despiérteme a las siete y media
despyer-te-me a las sye-te ee medya

Can I have my key? ¿Me da la llave?
me da la lya-be

We'll be back very late Volveremos muy tarde
bol-be-remos mooy tar-de

I want to stay an extra night Quiero quedarme una noche más
kyero kedar-me oona no-che mas

I shall be leaving tomorrow morning Me voy mañana por la mañana
me boy ma-nyana por la ma-nyana

bar
el bar
bar

desk
la recepción
re-thepthyon

lift
el ascensor
asthen-sor

lounge
el salón
salon

manager
el gerente
kheren-te

porter
el mozo
motho

reservation
la reserva
re-serba

restaurant
el restaurante
restow-ran-te

room service
el servicio de habitaciones
ser-beethyo de abee-tathyo-nes

stay
la estancia
estan-thya

TV lounge
la sala de televisión
sala de te-lebee-syon

Where do I check in my luggage?
¿Dónde tengo que facturar el equipaje?
don-de tengo ke faktoo-rar el e-keepa-khe

Where is the luggage from the London flight/train? ¿Dónde está el equipaje del vuelo/del tren de Londres?
don-de esta el e-keepa-khe del bwelo/del tren de lon-dres

Our luggage has not arrived Nuestro equipaje no ha llegado
nwestro e-keepa-khe no a lye-gado

My suitcase was damaged in transit Se me ha estropeado la maleta en el viaje
se me a estro-pe-a-do la ma-leta en el bya-khe

Where is the left luggage office?
¿Dónde está la consigna de equipajes?
don-de esta la kon-seegna de e-keepa-khes

Are there any luggage trolleys? ¿Hay carritos para el equipaje?
a-ee ka-rreetos para el e-keepa-khe

It's very heavy Pesa mucho
pesa moocho

Can you help me with my bags?
¿Puede ayudarme a llevar las maletas?
pwe-de a-yoodar-me a lyebar las ma-letas

Take my bags to a taxi Lléveme las maletas a un taxi
lye-be-me las ma-letas a oon taksee

I can manage this one myself Esta la puedo llevar yo
esta la pwedo lyebar yo

I sent my luggage on in advance He mandado el equipaje por adelantado
e man-dado el e-keepa-khe por a-delan-tado

baggage reclaim
la entrega de equipajes
en-trega de ekee-pa-khes

excess luggage
el exceso de equipaje
ex-theso de ekee-pa-khe

flight bag
la bolsa de viaje
bolsa de bya-khe

hand luggage
el equipaje de mano
ekee-pa-khe de mano

locker
el casillero de consigna
kasee-lyero de kon-seegna

luggage allowance
el equipaje permitido
ekee-pa-khe permee-teedo

luggage rack
la rejilla
re-kheelya

porter
el mozo
motho

trunk
el baúl
ba-ool

See also DIRECTIONS

Where can I buy a local map? ¿Dónde puedo comprar un mapa de la zona?
don-de pwedo komprar oon mapa de la thona

Have you got a town plan? ¿Tiene un plano de la ciudad?
tye-ne oon plano de la thyoodad

I want a street map of the city Quiero un plano callejero
kyero oon plano ka-lye-khero

I need a road map of ... Necesito un mapa de carreteras de ...
ne-the-seeto oon mapa de ka-rre-teras de ...

Can I get a map at the tourist office? ¿Podré comprar un mapa en la oficina de turismo?
po-dre komprar oon mapa en la ofee-theena de too-reesmo

Can you show me on the map? ¿Puede indicármelo en el mapa?
pwe-de eendee-kar-melo en el mapa

Do you have a guidebook in English? ¿Tiene alguna guía turística en inglés?
tye-ne al-goona gee-a toorees-teeka en een-gles

Do you have a guidebook to the cathedral? ¿Tiene alguna guía de la catedral?
tye-ne al-goona gee-a de la ka-tedral

I need an English-Spanish dictionary Necesito un diccionario inglés-español
ne-thesee-to oon deek-thyo-naryo een-gles-espa-nyol

See also BUYING, NUMBERS, PAYING

a pint of ...
medio litro de ...
medyo leetro de ...

a litre of ...
un litro de ...
oon leetro de ...

a kilo of ...
un kilo de ...
oon keelo de ...

a pound of ...
medio kilo de ...
medyo keelo de ...

100 grammes of ...
100 gramos de ...
thyen gramos de ...

half a kilo of ...
medio kilo de ...
medyo keelo de ...

a half-bottle of ...
media botella de ...
medya bo-telya de ...

a slice of ...
una loncha de ...
oona loncha de ...

a portion of ...
una ración de ...
oona rathyon de ...

a dozen ...
una docena de ...
oona do-thena de ...

1,000 pesetas' worth (of) ...
mil pesetas (de ...)
meel pe-setas (de ...)

a third
un tercio
oon terthyo

two thirds
dos tercios
dos terthyos

a quarter
un cuarto
oon kwarto

three quarters
tres cuartos
tres kwartos

ten per cent
el diez por ciento
el dyeth por thyento

more ...
más ...
mas ...

less ...
menos ...
menos ...

enough ...
bastante ...
bastan-te ...

double
el doble
el do-ble

twice
dos veces
dos be-thes

three times
tres veces
tres be-thes

See also EATING OUT, FOOD, WINES AND SPIRITS, WINE LIST

Starters - Entremeses

Alcachofas Artichokes
Anguila ahumada Smoked eel
Croquetas de gambas Prawn croquettes
Entremeses variados Mixed hors d'oeuvres
Fiambres Assorted cold meats and sausages
Patatas al ajillo Potatoes fried with garlic and parsley
Puntas de espárragos Asparagus tips
Tortilla de patatas Potato and onion omelette

Soups - Sopas

Caldo Clear soup or broth
Caldo gallego Clear soup with green vegetables, beans, pork
Gazpacho Gazpacho; cold soup made with tomatoes, onions,
cucumber, green peppers, soft breadcrumbs, garlic, oil
Potaje Thick vegetable soup
Potaje de garbanzos Thick chick pea soup
Sopa de ajo Spicy garlic soup with bread
Sopa de arroz Vegetable and rice soup
Sopa de pescado Fish soup
Sopa de puerros Leek and potato soup

Fish and Seafood - Pescado y Mariscos

Almejas Clams
Angulas Baby eels
Atún Fresh tuna fish
Bacalao al pil-pil Dried salt cod with a parsley sauce
Besugo a la parrilla Grilled sea bream
Bonito Bonito; a type of tunny fish
Boquerones fritos Fried (fresh) anchovies
Calamares en su tinta Squid cooked in their ink
Cangrejo Crab
Centollo Spider crab
Chipirones Baby squid
Escabeche de pescado Fish marinated in oil, garlic, herbs
Gambas a la plancha Grilled prawns
Langosta Lobster
Langostinos Crayfish
Lenguado a la parrilla Grilled sole
Mejillones a la marinera Mussels in white wine
Merluza en salsa verde Hake in parsley sauce
Percebes Barnacles
Platija Plaice
Pez espada Swordfish
Pulpo a la gallega Octopus with peppers and paprika
Salpicón de mariscos Prawns and lobster salad
Sardinas Sardines
Trucha a la navarra Trout marinated with wine and herbs
Zarzuela de mariscos Seafood casserole

Poultry - Aves

Codorniz Quail
Faisán Pheasant
Gallina Chicken
Pato a la naranja Duck in orange sauce
Pavo asado Roast turkey
Pechuga de pollo Breast of chicken
Perdiz Partridge
Pollo en pepitoria Chicken with almonds, garlic, herbs

Meat - Carne

Albóndigas Meatballs in tomato sauce
Butifarra Catalan sausage
Bistec Steak
Cabrito Kid
Callos a la madrileña Tripe in a spicy sauce with garlic and *chorizo*
Carne de vaca/cerdo/cordero Beef/pork/lamb
Cochinillo Suckling pig
Cocido Stew with chicken, beef and vegetables
Conejo guisado Rabbit stew
Chorizo Spicy red salami-type sausage
Escalope de ternera Veal escalope
Estofado de cordero Lamb stew
Filete (Fillet) steak
Jamón serrano Raw cured ham
Lengua Tongue
Liebre estofado con judías Hare stew with French beans
Lomo relleno Stuffed loin of pork
Manitas de cerdo Pig's trotters
Mollejas Sweetbreads
Morcilla Black pudding
Pierna de cordero Leg of lamb
Riñones al jerez Kidneys in a sherry sauce
Salchichas Sausages
Ternera Veal

Eggs - Huevos

Huevos a la flamenca Baked eggs with tomatoes, peas, peppers, asparagus, sausage, onions
Huevos fritos Fried eggs
Huevos al plato Baked eggs
Huevos revueltos Scrambled eggs
Tortilla francesa Plain omelette
Tortilla de patatas Potato and onion omelette

Rice Dishes - Arroz

Arroz blanco Boiled (white) rice
Arroz a la cubana Boiled rice with fried egg and bananas
Paella Rice dish with chicken, shellfish, garlic, saffron and vegetables

Salads and Vegetables - Ensaladas y Verduras

Acelgas Chard
Berenjenas fritas Fried aubergines
Ensalada mixta Mixed salad
Fabada Bean stew with black pudding, ham and vegetables
Menestra de legumbres A sort of vegetable stew
Patatas fritas Chips
Puerros en ensalada Boiled leeks in vinaigrette
Pisto Sautéed peppers, onions, aubergines, tomatoes, garlic
Remolacha en ensalada Beetroot in vinaigrette

Cheeses - Quesos

Queso de bola A round mild cheese
Queso de Burgos Soft fresh curd cheese from Burgos
Queso de cabra Goat's milk cheese
Queso fresco Curd cheese
Queso manchego Hard sheep's cheese from La Mancha
Queso de oveja Sheep's milk cheese
Queso del país Local cheese
Requesón Curd cheese from Catalonia
Queso de Roncal smoked hard cheese made from sheep's milk

Desserts - Postres

Arroz con leche Rice pudding flavoured with cinnamon
Bizcocho Sponge cake
Churros Fritters
Crema catalana Baked custard topped with caramelized sugar
Cuajada Junket
Flan Caramel custard
Helado Ice-cream
Leche frita Thick slices of custard fried in breadcrumbs
Leche merengada Milk and egg sorbet
Manzanas rellenas Stuffed apples
Tocino de cielo A rich, thick caramel custard
Tortilla al ron Sweet rum omelette
Turrón Nougat made with almonds, honey and egg white
Yema Dessert made of egg yolks, brandy and sugar

Understanding the menu

al ajillo in garlic sauce
ahumado smoked
asado roasted
a la chilindrón with tomatoes, peppers, onions
empanado fried in breadcrumbs
estofado braised/stewed
frito fried
gratinado with a cheese topping
al horno oven-baked
a la parrilla/a la plancha grilled
rehogado fried in oil with garlic and vinegar
en salsa blanca in a white sauce

I haven't enough money No tengo suficiente dinero
no tengo soofee-thyen-te dee-nero

Have you any change? ¿Tiene cambio?
tye-ne kambyo

Can you change a 1,000 peseta note? ¿Puede cambiarme un billete de mil pesetas?
pwe-de kambyar-me oon bee-lye-te de meel pe-setas

I'd like to change these traveller's cheques Querría cambiar estos cheques de viaje
kerree-a kambyar estos che-kes de bya-khe

I want to change some pesetas into pounds Quiero cambiar pesetas en libros
kyero kambyar pe-setas en leebros

What is the rate for sterling/dollars? ¿A cómo está la libra esterlina/el dólar?
a komo esta la leebra ester-leena/el dolar

I'd like to cash a cheque with my Eurocheque card Querría hacer efectivo un cheque con la tarjeta de Eurocheque
kerree-a a-ther efek-teebo oon che-ke kon la tar-kheta de e-ooro-che-ke

Can I get a cash advance with my credit card? ¿Puedo obtener dinero en efectivo con mi tarjeta de crédito?
pwedo ob-tener dee-nero en efek-teebo kon mee tar-kheta de cre-deeto

I should like to transfer some money from my bank in ... Querría hacer una transferencia de mi banco de ...
kerree-a a-ther oona trans-feren-thya de mee banko de ...

bureau de change
el cambio
kambyo

cash
el dinero
dee-nero

cheque book
el talonario
talo-naryo

currency
la moneda
mo-neda

exchange rate
el tipo de cambio
teepo de kambyo

notes
los billetes (de banco)
bee-lye-tes (de banko)

post office
la oficina de correos
ofee-theena de ko-rre-os

purse
el monedero
mo-ne-dero

wallet
la cartera
kar-tera

See also EATING OUT, ENTERTAINMENT

What is there to do in the evenings? ¿Qué se puede hacer
por las noches?
*ke se **pwe**-de a-**ther** por las **no**-ches*

Where can we go to see a cabaret/go to dance? ¿Dónde
podemos ir a ver un cabaret/ir a bailar?
don**-de po-**demos** eer a ber oon kaba-**re**/eer a ba-ee-**lar

Are there any good night clubs/discos? ¿Hay algún
nightclub bueno/alguna discoteca buena?
*a-ee al**goon** night-kloob **bwe**no/al-**goona** deesko-**teka bwena***

How do we get to the casino? ¿Cómo se puede ir al casino?
komo** se **pwe**-de eer al ka-**seeno

Do we need to be members? ¿Hace falta ser socio?
*a-the **falta** ser **sothyo***

How much does it cost to get in? ¿Cuánto cuesta la entrada?
kwanto kwesta** la en-**trada

We'd like to reserve two seats for tonight Querríamos
reservar dos butacas para esta noche
*kerree-amos reser-**bar** dos boo-**takas** para esta **no**-che*

Is there a bar/a restaurant? ¿Hay bar/restaurante?
*a-ee bar/restow-**ran**-te*

What time does the show/concert begin? ¿A qué hora
empieza el espectáculo/el concierto?
*a ke **o**-ra em-**pyetha** el espek-**takoo**-lo/el kon-**thyerto***

How long does the performance last? ¿Cuánto dura la
representación?
kwanto **doo**ra la re-presen-**tathyon

Which film is on at the cinema? ¿Qué película ponen en el
cine?
*ke pe**lee**-koola **po**-nen en el **thee**-ne*

Can we get there by bus/taxi? ¿Podemos ir en autobús/en
taxi?
*po-**demos** eer en owto-**boos**/en **taksee***

See also ROAD SIGNS

Abierto
Open

Acceso a los andenes
To the trains

Agua potable
Drinking water

Alto
Stop

Ascensor
Lift

Autoservicio
Self-service

Caballeros
Gentlemen, Men

Caja
Cash desk

Caliente
Hot

Cerrado
Closed

Completo
No vacancies

Consigna
Left luggage

Damas
Ladies

Degustación
Sampling
  (of wine etc)

Empuje
Push

Entrada
Entrance

Entrada libre
No obligation
to buy

Frío
Cold

Fumadores
Smokers, Smoking

Información
Information,
Enquiries

Libre
Free, Vacant

No funciona
Out of order

Ocupado
Engaged

Oficina de Información y Turismo
Tourist
Information
Office

Planta baja
Ground floor

Plazas libres
Vacancies

Privada
Private

Prohibida la entrada/ Prohibido el paso
Keep out, No entry

Prohibido bañarse
No bathing

Prohibido fumar
No smoking

Prohibido pisar la hierba
Do not walk
on the grass

Rebajas
Sale

Salida
Exit

Salida de emergencia
Emergency exit

Se alquila
For hire, To rent

Señoras
Ladies

Se vende
For sale

Sótano
Basement

Taquilla
Ticket office

Tirad
Pull

See also MEASUREMENTS AND QUANTITIES

0	cero *thero*	13	trece *tre-the*	50	cincuenta *theen-kwenta*
1	uno *oono*	14	catorce *kator-the*	60	sesenta *se-senta*
2	dos *dos*	15	quince *keen-the*	70	setenta *se-tenta*
3	tres *tres*	16	dieciséis *dyethee-se-ees*	80	ochenta *o-chenta*
4	cuatro *kwatro*	17	diecisiete *dyethee-sye-te*	90	noventa *no-benta*
5	cinco *theenko*	18	dieciocho *dyethee-o-cho*	100	cien *thyen*
6	seis *se-ees*	19	diecinueve *dyethee-nwe-be*	110	ciento diez *thyento dyeth*
7	siete *sye-te*	20	veinte *be-een-te*	200	doscientos *dos-thyentos*
8	ocho *o-cho*	21	veintiuno *be-eentee-oo-no*	300	trescientos *tres-thyentos*
9	nueve *nwe-be*	22	veintidós *be-eentee-dos*	500	quinientos *kee-nyentos*
10	diez *dyeth*	23	veintitrés *be-eentee-tres*	1,000	mil *meel*
11	once *on-the*	30	treinta *tre-eenta*	2,000	dos mil *dos meel*
12	doce *do-the*	40	cuarenta *kwa-renta*	1,000,000	un millón *oon meelyon*

1st	primero *pree-mero*	6th	sexto *seksto*
2nd	segundo *se-goondo*	7th	séptimo *sep-teemo*
3rd	tercero *ter-thero*	8th	octavo *ok-tabo*
4th	cuarto *kwarto*	9th	noveno *no-beno*
5th	quinto *keento*	10th	décimo *de-theemo*

See also COMPLAINTS, EATING OUT, MENUS, PAYING, WINES AND
SPIRITS

Do you have a set menu? ¿Tienen
menú?
tye-nen menoo

We will have the menu at 600 pesetas
Tráiganos el plato del día de 600 pesetas
*tra-eega-nos el plato deh dee-a de se-ees-
thyentas pe-setas*

May we see the wine list, please? ¿Nos
trae la carta de vinos, por favor?
nos tra-e la karta de beenos por fabor

What do you recommend? ¿Qué
recomienda usted?
ke reko-myenda oos-ted

Is there a local speciality? ¿Hay alguna
especialidad local?
a-ee al-goona es-pethya-leedad lokal

How is this dish served? ¿Con qué se
sirve este plato?
kon ke se seer-be es-te plato

How do I eat this? ¿Cómo se come esto?
komo se ko-me esto

What is in this dish? ¿Qué tiene este
plato?
ke tye-ne es-te plato

Are the vegetables included? ¿Va
incluida la verdura?
ba eenkloo-eeda la ber-doora

Rare/medium rare/well done please
Poco/medianamente/muy hecho, por favor
*poko/medya-namen-te/mooy e-cho por
fabor*

We'd like a dessert/some coffee, please
¿Nos trae el postre/café, por favor?
nos tra-e el pos-tre/ka-fe por fabor

bill	
la cuenta	
kwenta	
course	
el plato	
plato	
cover charge	
el precio del	
cubierto	
prethyo del koo-	
byerto	
meal	
la comida	
ko-meeda	
order	
la orden	
or-den	
service	
el servicio	
ser-beethyo	
table	
la mesa	
mesa	
that one	
ése (ésa)	
e-se (esa)	
this one	
éste (ésta)	
es-te (esta)	
waiter	
el camarero	
kama-rero	
waitress	
la camarera	
kama-rera	

See also BUYING, MONEY

Can I have the bill, please? La factura, por favor
la fak-toora por fabor

Is service/tax included? ¿Incluye el servicio/los impuestos?
eenkloo-ye el ser-beethyo/los eempwestos

What does that come to? ¿Cuánto hace eso?
kwanto a-the e-so

How much is that? ¿Cuánto es eso?
kwanto es e-so

Do I pay a deposit? ¿Tengo que pagar un depósito?
tengo ke pagar oon depo-seeto

Can I pay by credit card/cheque? ¿Puedo pagar con tarjeta de crédito/con un cheque?
pwedo pagar kon tar-kheta de kre-deeto/kon oon che-ke

Do you accept traveller's cheques? ¿Aceptan cheques de viaje?
a-theptan che-kes de bya-khe

I don't have enough in cash No tengo suficiente en metálico
no tengo soofee-thyen-te en meta-leeko

You've given me the wrong change Se ha equivocado en el cambio
se a e-keebo-kado en el kambyo

I'd like a receipt, please ¿Me da un recibo, por favor?
me da oon re-theebo por fabor

Can I have an itemized bill? ¿Me da una factura detallada?
me da oon fak-toora deta-lyada

cash desk
la caja
kakha

cashier
el cajero/la cajera
ka-khero/ka-khera

charge
el precio
prethyo

cheaper
más barato
mas ba-rato

cheque card
la tarjeta de identidad bancaria
tar-kheta de eeden-teedad ban-karya

discount
el descuento
des-kwento

expensive
caro
karo

in advance
por adelantado
por a-delan-tado

payment
el pago
pago

reduction
la rebaja
re-bakha

signature
la firma
feerma

till
la caja
kakha

My name is ... Me llamo ...
me lyamo ...

My date of birth is ... Mi fecha de nacimiento es el ...
mee fecha de nathee-myento es el ...

My address is ... Mi dirección es ...
mee deerek-thyon es ...

I come from Britain/America Soy británico/americano
soy breeta-neeko/a-meree-kano

I live in ... Vivo en ...
beebo en ...

My passport/driving licence number is ... El número de mi pasaporte/permiso de conducir es ...
el noo-mero de mee pasa-por-te/per-meeso de kondoo-theer es ...

My blood group is ... Mi grupo sanguíneo es ...
mee groopo san-gee-ne-o es ...

I work in an office/a factory Trabajo en una oficina/una fábrica
tra-bakho en oona ofee-theena/oona fa-breeka

I am a secretary/manager Soy secretaria/gerente
soy se-kreta-rya/kheren-te

I'm here on holiday/business He venido de vacaciones/de negocios
e be-needo de baka-thyo-nes/de nego-thyos

There are four of us Somos cuatro
somos kwatro

My daughter/son is 6 Mi hija/mi hijo tiene seis años
mee eekha/mee eekho tye-ne se-ees a-nyos

blind
ciego
thyego

child
el niño/la niña
neenyo/neenya

deaf
sordo
sordo

disabled
minusválido
meenoos-balee-do

English
inglés/inglesa
een-gles/een-glesa

husband
el marido
ma-reedo

Irish
irlandés/irlandesa
eerlan-des/eerlan-desa

Scottish
escocés/escocesa
esko-thes/esko-thesa

student
el/la estudiante
estoo-dyan-te

Welsh
galés/galesa
ga-les/ga-lesa

wife
la esposa
es-posa

See also CAR PARTS, DRIVING ABROAD, PAYING

20 litres of 2 star Veinte litros de normal
be-een-te leetros de normal

1,000 pesetas (worth) of 4 star Mil
pesetas de super
meel pe-setas de soo-per

Fill it up please Lleno, por favor
lyeno por fabor

Check the oil/the water Revíseme el
aceite/el agua
rebee-se-me el a-the-ee-te/el a-gwa

Top up the windscreen washers
Relléneme el depósito del limpiaparabrisas
*relye-ne-me el depo-seeto del leempya-
para-breesas*

Could you clean the windscreen?
¿Podría limpiarme el parabrisas?
podree-a leempyar-me el para-breesas

A can of oil Una lata de aceite
oona lata de a-the-ee-te

Where's the air line? ¿Dónde está el
aire?
don-de esta el a-ee-re

Can I have a can of petrol? ¿Me de una
lata de gasolina?
me da oona lata de gaso-leena

Is there a telephone/a lavatory? ¿Hay
teléfono/servicios?
a-ee te-lefo-no/serbee-thyos

How do I use the car wash? ¿Cómo
funciona el lavado automático?
*komo foon-thyona el la-bado owto-matee-
ko*

Can I pay by credit card? ¿Puedo pagar
con tarjeta de crédito?
pwedo pagar kon tar-kheta de cre-deeto

attendant
el empleado
em-ple-a-do

diesel
el gas-oil
gaso-eel

distilled water
el agua destilada
a-gwa destee-lada

garage
el garaje
gara-khe

hose
la manguera
man-gera

petrol pump
el surtidor de
gasolina
*soortee-dor de
gaso-leena*

petrol station
la estación de
servicio
*esta-thyon de ser-
beethyo*

tyre pressure
la presión de los
neumáticos
*presyon de los ne-
oo-matee-kos*

I need a colour/black and white film for this camera Necesito un carrete en color/en blanco y negro para esta cámara
ne-thesee-to oon ka-rre-te en kolor/en blanko ee negro para esta ka-mara

It is for prints/slides Es para copias en papel/para diapositivas
es para kopyas en pa-pel/para dee-apo-seetee-bas

Have you got some flash cubes for this camera? ¿Tiene cubos de flash para esta cámara?
tye-ne koobos de flash para esta ka-mara

There's something wrong with my cine-camera Mi cámara tomavistas no va bien
mee ka-mara toma-beestas no ba byen

The film/shutter has jammed La película está atascada/El obturador está atascado
la pelee-koola esta atas-kada/el obtoo-rador esta atas-kado

The rewind mechanism does not work No funciona el rebobinado
no foon-thyona el rebo-beena-do

Can you develop this film, please? ¿Puede revelar esta película, por favor?
pwe-de re-belar esta pelee-koola por fabor

When will the photos be ready? ¿Para cuándo estarán las fotos?
para kwando esta-ran las fotos

Can I take photos in here? ¿Puedo hacer fotos aqui?
pwedo a-ther fotos a-kee

Would you take a photo of us, please? ¿Podría hacernos una foto, por favor?
podree-a a-thernos oona foto por fabor

---

cartridge
el cartucho
kar-toocho

cassette
la cassette
kaset

exposure meter
el fotómetro
foto-metro

flash
el flash
flash

flash bulb
la bombilla de flash
bom-beelya de flash

lens
la lente
len-te

lens cover
la tapa de la lente
tapa de la len-te

movie camera
la cámara de cine
ka-mara de thee-ne

negative
el negativo
nega-teebo

reel
el carrete
ka-rre-te

tripod
el tripode
treepo-de

See also ACCIDENTS, CUSTOMS AND PASSPORTS, EMERGENCIES
Police in Spain have the power to impose on-the-spot fines for
traffic offences. A 20 percent discount is usually allowed for
immediate payment.

We should call the police Deberíamos
llamar a la policía
de-be-ree-amos lyamar a la polee-thee-a

Where is the police station? ¿Dónde
está la comisaría (de policía)?
don-de esta la komee-saree-a (de polee-thee-a)

My car has been broken into Me han
forzado la cerradura del coche
me an for-thado la therra-doora del ko-che

I've been robbed Me han robado
me an ro-bado

I have had an accident He tenido un
accidente
e te-needo oon akthee-den-te

How much is the fine? ¿Cuánto es la
multa?
kwanto es la moolta

How do I pay it? ¿Cómo la pago?
komo la pago

Can I pay at a police station? ¿Puedo
pagarlo en una comisaría?
pwedo pagar-lo en oona komee-saree-a

I don't have my driving licence on me
No llevo mi permiso de conducir
no lyebo mee per-meeso de kondoo-theer

I'm very sorry, officer Lo siento mucho,
agente
lo syento moocho a-khen-te

I didn't know the regulations No
conocía las normas
no kono-thee-a las normas

car number
la matrícula
matree-koola

documents
los documentos
dokoo-mentos

green card
la carta verde
karta ber-de

insurance certificate
el certificado de
seguros
*thertee-feeka-do de
se-gooros*

lawyer
el abogado
abo-gado

police car
el coche patrulla
ko-che pa-troolya

policeman
un policía
polee-thee-a

traffic offence
la infracción de
tráfico
*eenfrak-thyon de
tra-feeko*

traffic warden
el guardia de
tráfico
gwardya de tra-feeko

If you only want stamps it's simplest to get them in a tobacconist's shop (*estanco*). Spanish post offices have separate counters for different services. You don't phone from the post office but from the telephone exchange (*telefónica*).

How much is a letter to England/ America? ¿Qué franqueo llevan las cartas para Inglaterra/para los Estados Unidos?
*ke fran-**ke**-o **l**yeban las **k**artas para eengla-terra/para los esta-dos oonee-dos*

I'd like six stamps for postcards to Great Britain, please ¿Me da sellos para enviar seis postales a Gran Bretaña, por favor?
*me da **se**lyos para en**byar** se-ees posta-les a gran bre-**tanya** por fa**bor***

Twelve 35 peseta stamps please Doce sellos de treinta y cinco pesetas, por favor
do**-the **se**lyos de **tre**-eenta ee **theen**ko pe-setas por fa**bor

I want to send a telegram to ... Quiero mandar un telegrama a ...
***kye**ro man**dar** oon te-**legra**-ma a ...*

When will it arrive? ¿Cuándo llegará?
kwan**do lye**ga-ra

How much will it cost? ¿Cuánto va a costar?
kwan**to ba a kos**tar

Do I have to fill in a form? ¿Tengo que rellenar un impreso?
ten**go ke re-lye**nar** oon eem-**preso

I want to draw some money out of my Giro account Quiero sacar dinero de mi cuenta de Giro Bank
***kye**ro sa**kar** dee-**ne**ro de mee **kwen**ta de giro bank*

air mail
por avión/por correo aéreo
*por a-**byon**/por ko-**rre**-o a-e-re-o*

clerk
el empleado
*em-ple-**a**-do*

counter
la caja
***ka**kha*

express
por correo urgente
*por ko-**rre**-o oor**khen**-te*

money order
el giro postal
***khee**ro postal*

parcel
el paquete
*pa-**ke**-te*

post office
la oficina de correos
*ofee-**thee**na de ko-**rre**-os*

postage
el franqueo
*fran-**ke**-o*

registered
certificado
*thertee-**feeka**-do*

reply coupon
el cupón-respuesta
*koo**pon**-res-**pwes**ta*

See also ACCIDENTS, COMPLAINTS, EMERGENCIES, POLICE

Can you help me, please? ¿Puede ayudarme, por favor?
pwe-de a-yoodar-me por fabor

What is the matter? ¿Qué pasa?
ke pasa

I am in trouble Estoy en un apuro
estoy en oon a-pooro

I don't understand No entiendo
no en-tyendo

Do you speak English? ¿Habla usted inglés?
a-bla oos-ted een-gles

Please repeat that ¿Puede repetir eso, por favor?
pwe-de re-peteer e-so por fabor

I have run out of money Me he quedado sin dinero
me e ke-dado seen dee-nero

My son is lost Mi hijo se ha perdido
mee ee-kho se a per-deedo

I have lost my way Me he perdido
me e per-deedo

I have forgotten my passport Se me ha olvidado el pasaporte
se me a olbee-dado el pasa-por-te

Please give me my passport back ¿Me devuelve el
pasaporte, por favor?
me debwel-be el pasa-por-te por fabor

Where is the British Consulate? ¿Dónde está el Consulado
Británico?
don-de esta el konsoo-lado breeta-neeko

In the pronunciation system used in this book, Spanish sounds are represented by spellings of the nearest possible sounds in English. Hence, when you read out the pronunciation - the line in *italics* after each phrase or word - sound the letters as if you were reading an English word. The syllable to be stressed is shown in **heavy italics**. The following notes should help you:

	REMARKS	EXAMPLE	PRONOUNCED
e	midway between *gate* and *get*	puede	*pwe*-de
o	midway between *goat* and *got*	como	*komo*
y	as in *yet*	tiene	*tye*-ne
th	as in *thick*	centro	*then*tro
kh	as in Scottish *loch*	gente	*khen*-te
ly	as in *million*	calle	*ka-lye*
ny	as in *onion*	niño	*neenyo*

Spelling in Spanish is very regular and, with a little practice, you will soon be able to pronounce Spanish words from their spelling alone. The only letters which are unlike English are:

v,w	as *b* in *bed*	curva	*koorba*
c	before *a,o,u* as in *cat*	calle	*ka-lye*
	before *e,i* as *th* in *thin*	centro	*then*tro
g	before *a,o,u* as in *got*	gato	*gato*
	before *e,i* as *ch* in *loch*	gente	*khen*-te
h	silent	hombre	*om-bre*
j	as *ch* in *loch*	jueves	*khwe*-bes
ll	as *lli* in *million*	calle	*ka-lye*
n	as *ni* in *onion*	niño	*neenyo*
z	as *th* in *thin*	zumo	*thoomo*

The letter *r* is always rolled; the double *r* is rolled even more strongly. Spanish vowels are single sounds: when you find two together, pronounce both of them in quick succession as in **aceite** *a-the-ee-te*.

Latin American countries each have their own Day of Independence; national saint's days are public holidays.

New Year's Day	January 1st
Epiphany	January 6th
St Joseph's Day	March 19th
Maundy Thursday	
Good Friday	
Corpus Christi	
Labour Day	May 1st
St James's Day	July 25th (*Spain*)
Assumption	August 15th
Hispanidad	October 12th
All Saint's Day	November 1st
Immaculate Conception	December 8th
Christmas Day	December 25th

See also LUGGAGE, TRAIN TRAVEL

On main routes it is a good idea to reserve your seat in advance. A supplement is payable on some of the luxury trains like the TALGO or the TER. For overnight travel you can book a sleeper or couchette. Children under 3 travel free; 3 to 7's pay half-fare. Smoking is only allowed in the corridors of trains, not in the compartments.

What time are the trains to ...? ¿Cuál es el horario de los trenes a ...?
*kwal es el o-ra**ryo** de los **tre**-nes a ...*

When is the next train to ...? ¿A qué hora sale el próximo tren para ...?
*a ke **o**-ra **sa**-le el **prok**-seemo tren para ...*

When does it arrive? ¿A qué hora llega?
*a ke **o**-ra **lye**ga*

Do I have to change? ¿Tengo que hacer transbordo?
*tengo ke a-**ther** trans-**bordo***

A first class ticket to ..., return Un billete de primera para ..., de ida y vuelta
*oon bee**lye**-te de pree-**me**ra para ... de **ee**-da de **bwel**ta*

A second class single to ... Un billete de segunda para ...
*oon bee**lye**-te de se-**goon**da para ...*

Is there a supplement to pay? ¿Hay que pagar algún suplemento?
*a-ee ke pagar al**goon** soo-ple**men**-to*

I want to reserve a couchette/sleeper Quiero reservar una litera/un coche-cama
***kye**ro reser-**bar** oona lee-**te**ra/oon ko-che-**ka**ma*

Which platform for the train to ...? ¿Cuál es el andén para (el tren de) ...?
*kwal es el an-**den** para (el tren de) ...*

arrival	la llegada *lye-**ga**da*
buffet	la cafetería *ka-fe-te**ree**-a*
departure	la salida *sa-**lee**da*
guard	el jefe de tren *khe-fe de tren*
half fare	el medio billete *medyo bee-**lye**-te*
left luggage	la consigna *kon-**seeg**na*
reservation	la reserva *re-**ser**ba*
ticket office	el despacho de billetes/la taquilla *des-**pa**cho de bee-**lye**-tes/ta-**kee**lya*
timetable board	el horario *o-**ra**ryo*
waiting room	la sala de espera *sala de es-**pe**ra*

See also ACCIDENTS, BREAKDOWNS, EMERGENCIES

I have broken a glass/the window He
roto un vaso/la ventana
e roto oon baso/la ben-tana

**There is a hole in my shoe/these
trousers** Mi zapato/este pantalón está
agujereado
mee tha-pato/es-te panta-lon esta agoo-khe-re-a-do

This is broken/torn Esto está
roto/rasgado
esto esta roto/ras-gado

Can you repair this? ¿Puede arreglar
esto?
pwe-de a-rreglar esto

Can you do it quickly? ¿Puede
hacérmelo rápido?
pwe-de a-ther-melo ra-peedo

When can you get it done by? ¿Para
cuándo me lo puede tener?
para kwando me lo pwe-de te-ner

I need some adhesive tape/a safety pin
Necesito cinta adhesiva/un imperdible
ne-thesee-to theenta a-desee-ba/oon eemper-dee-ble

The stitching has come undone Se ha
descosido la costura
se a desko-seedo la kos-toora

Can you reheel these shoes? ¿Puede
poner tapas a estos zapatos?
pwe-de po-ner tapas a estos tha-patos

The handle has come off Se le ha caído
el asa
se a ka-eedo el a-sa

button
el botón
boton

glue
la cola
kola

hammer
el martillo
mar-teelyo

nail
el clavo
klabo

pin
el alfiler
alfee-ler

screw
el tornillo
tor-neelyo

screwdriver
el destornillador
destor-neelya-dor

string
la cuerda
kwerda

tape
la cinta
theenta

temporary
provisional
probee-syonal

See also DRIVING ABROAD, ROAD SIGNS, WEATHER

Is there a route that avoids the traffic? ¿Hay algún otro camino que evite los atascos?
a-ee algoon o-tro ka-meeno ke e-bee-te los a-taskos

Is the traffic heavy on the motorway? ¿Hay mucho tráfico en la autopista?
a-ee moocho tra-feeko en la owto-peesta

What is causing this hold-up? ¿A qué se debe este atasco?
a ke se de-be es-te a-tasko

When will the road be clear? ¿Cuándo estará despejada la carretera?
kwando esta-ra des-pekha-da la ka-rre-tera

Is there a detour? ¿Hay algún desvío?
a-ee algoon desbee-o

Is the road to ... snowed up? ¿Está bloqueada por la nieve la carretera para ir a ...?
esta blo-ke-ada por la nye-be la ka-rre-tera para eer a ...

Is the pass/tunnel open? ¿Está abierto el puerto/el túnel?
esta a-byerta el pwerto/el toonel

Do I need chains? ¿Hacen falta cadenas?
a-then falta ka-denas

accident
el accidente (de circulación)
akthee-den-te (de theerkoo-lathyon)

black ice
el hielo
yelo

fog
la niebla
nyebla

frost
la escarcha
es-karcha

heavy rain
la lluvia fuerte
lyoobya fwer-te

road conditions
las condiciones de la circulación
kondeethyo-nes de la theerkoo-lathyon

road works
las obras
o-bras

tailback
la cola
kola

traffic jam
el embotellamiento
embo-telya-myento

weather conditions
el estado del tiempo
es-tado del tyempo

See also DRIVING ABROAD, NOTICES

Aduana
Customs

Alto
Stop

Aparcamiento
Parking

Atención
Caution

Autopista (de peaje)
(Toll) motorway

Calzada deteriorada
Uneven road surface

Callejón sin salida
No through road

Camino cerrado
Road closed

Ceda el paso
Give way

Centro urbano/ciudad
City/town centre

Circule a su derecha
Keep right

Conducir por la derecha/la izquierda
Drive on the right/the left

Curva peligrosa
Dangerous bend

Dejar libre la salida
Exit - keep clear

Desembocadura de una calle
Road junction

Despacio
Slow

Desviación/Desvío
Diversion

Dirección prohibida
No entry

Dirección única
One-way street

Disminuir la marcha
Reduce speed

Encender las luces
Switch on headlights

Entrada
Way in

Escuela
School

Estacionamiento
Parking

Fin de la prohibición de estacionamiento
End of parking restrictions

Firme deslizante
Slippery road

Fuerte declive
Steep hill

Gravilla
Loose chippings

¡Pare!
Stop

Paso a nivel
Level crossing

Paso prohibido
No right of way

Paso protegido
Priority

Peaje
Toll

Peatones
Pedestrians

Peligro
Danger

Prioridad a la derecha
Priority to the right

Prohibido aparcar/detenerse
No parking

Respetar la precedencia
Give way

Salida
Way out

Vehículos pesados
Heavy goods vehicles

Velocidad limitada
Speed limit

See also CLEANING, COMPLAINTS, HOTEL DESK, TELEPHONE

Come in! ¡Pase!
pa-se

We'd like breakfast/a bottle of wine in our room ¿Nos trae
el desayuno/una botella de vino a nuestra habitación?
*nos tra-e el desa-yoono/oona bo-telya de beeno a nwestra
abee-tathyon*

Put it on my bill Póngalo en mi cuenta
ponga-lo en mee kwenta

I'd like an outside line, please ¿Me da línea para llamar, por
favor?
me da lee-ne-a para lyamar por fabor

I have lost my key He perdido la llave
e per-deedo la lya-be

I have locked myself out of my room Se me ha quedado la
llave dentro de la habitación
se me a keda-do la lya-be dentro de la abee-tathyon

Where is the socket for my electric razor? ¿Dónde está el
enchufe para la máquina de afeitar?
don-de esta el enchoo-fe para la ma-keena de a-fe-ee-tar

What's the voltage? ¿De cuánto es la corriente?
de kwanto es la korryen-te

I need a hairdryer/an iron Necesito un secador de pelo/una
plancha
ne-thesee-to oon seka-dor de pelo/oona plancha

May I have an extra blanket/pillow? ¿Puede darme otra
manta/almohada más?
pwe-de dar-me o-tra manta/almo-a-da mas

The TV/radio does not work No funciona el televisor/la radio
no foonthyo-na el te-lebee-sor/la radyo

Please send someone to collect my luggage ¿Me manda a
alguien para recoger mi equipaje, por favor?
me manda a algyen para reko-kher mee e-keepa-khe por fabor

We are going aboard now Nos embarcamos ahora
nos embar-kamos a-o-ra

The wind is getting up Se está levantado el viento
se esta leban-tado el byento

It's blowing hard from the north Sopla viento fuerte del norte
sopla byento fwer-te del nor-te

It's flat calm Hace calma
a-the kalma

We'll have to use the engine Tendremos que usar el motor
ten-dremos ke oosar el motor

When is the weather forecast? ¿Cuándo es el parte meteorológico?
kwando es el par-te me-te-oro-lokhee-ko

We'll anchor here for the night Anclaremos aqui para pasar la noche
ankla-remos a-kee para pasar la no-che

Please take my mooring line Coge mi amarra por favor
ko-khe mee a-marra por fabor

I'm feeling seasick Me estoy mareando
me estoy ma-re-ando

anchor
la ancla
ankla

boom
la botavara
bota-bara

bow
la proa
pro-a

dinghy
el barco a vela
barko a be-la

harbour
el puerto
pwerto

jib
el foque
fo-ke

mast
el mástil
masteel

propeller
la hélice
e-lee-the

rudder
el timón
teemon

sail
la vela
bela

sheet
la escota
es-kota

stern
la popa
popa

We've booked an apartment in the name of ... Tenemos reservado un apartamento a nombre de ...
te-ne-mos reser-ba-do oon apar-tamen-to a nom-bre de ...

Which is the key for the front door? ¿Cuál es la llave de la puerta de entrada?
kwal es la lya-be de la pwerta de en-trada

Please show us around ¿Nos enseña la casa, por favor?
nos en-senya la kasa por fabor

Where is the electricity meter/the water heater? ¿Dónde está el contador de la luz/el calentador del agua?
don-de esta el konta-dor de la looth/el konta-dor del a-gwa

How does the heating/the shower work? ¿Cómo funciona la calefacción/la ducha?
komo foon-thyona la ka-lefak-thyon/la doocha

Which day does the cleaner come? ¿Qué día vienen a limpiar?
ke dee-a bye-nen a leempyar

Is there any spare bedding? ¿Tiene más ropa de cama?
tye-ne mas ropa de kama

A fuse has blown Se han fundido los plomos
se an foon-deedo los plomos

Where can I contact you? ¿Dónde puedo ponerme en contacto con usted?
don-de pwedo poner-me en kon-takto kon oos-ted

---

bathroom
el cuarto de baño
kwarto de banyo

bedroom
el dormitorio
dormee-toryo

cooker
la cocina
ko-theena

electricity
la electricidad
elek-treethee-dad

fridge
el frigorífico
freego-reefee-ko

gas
el gas
gas

heater
el radiador
radya-dor

light
la luz
looth

living room
el cuarto de estar
kwarto de estar

kitchen
la cocina
ko-theena

sheet
la plancha
plancha

toilet
el wáter/el lavabo
bater/la-babo

See also BUYING, PAYING

Where is the main shopping area?
¿Dónde está el centro comercial?
don-de esta el thentro komer-thyal

Where are the big stores? ¿Dónde están
los grandes almacenes?
don-de estan los gran-des alma-the-nes

What time do the shops close? ¿A qué
hora cierran las tiendas?
a ke o-ra thyerran las tyendas

How much does that cost? ¿Cuánto
cuesta eso?
kwanto kwesta e-so

How much is it per kilo/per metre? ¿A
cuánto es el kilo/el metro?
a kwanto es el keelo/el metro

Can I try it on? ¿Puedo probármelo?
pwedo probar-melo

**Where is the shoe/menswear
department?** ¿Dónde está la sección de
zapatería/de caballeros?
*don-de esta la sekthyon de thapa-teree-
a/de kaba-lyeros*

I'm looking for a gift for my wife
Busco un regalo para mi mujer
boosko oon re-galo para mee moo-kher

I'm just looking Sólo estoy mirando
solo estoy mee-rando

**Have you anything suitable for a 5-
year-old boy?** ¿Tiene algo para un niño
de cinco años?
*tye-ne algo para oon neenyo de theenko
a-nyos*

Can I have a carrier bag please? ¿Me
da una bolsa, por favor?
me da oona bolsa por fabor

cash desk
la caja
kakha

changing room
el probador
proba-dor

closed
cerrado
the-rrado

exit
la salida
sa-leeda

market
el mercado
mer-kado

open
abierto
a-byerto

paper bag
la bolsa/el saco (de
papel)
*bolsa/sako (de pa-
pel)*

shopping bag
la bolsa (de
compras)
bolsa (de kompras)

stall
el puesto
pwesto

window
el escaparate
eska-para-te

See also MAPS AND GUIDES, TRIPS AND EXCURSIONS

What is there to see here? ¿Qué cosas interesantes se pueden ver aquí? *ke kosas een-te-resan-tes se pwe-den ber a-kee*	**guide book** la guía turística *gee-a toorees-teeka*
Excuse me, how do I get to the cathedral? Por favor, ¿por dónde se va a la catedral? *por fabor por don-de se ba a la ka-tedral*	**map** el mapa *mapa*
Where is the museum/the main square? ¿Dónde está el museo/la plaza mayor? *don-de esta el moo-se-o/la platha mayor*	**park** el parque *par-ke* **souvenirs** los recuerdos *re-kwerdos*
What time does the guided tour begin? ¿A qué hora empieza la visita con guía? *a ke ora em-pyetha el bee-seeta kon gee-a*	**street plan** el plano (de la ciudad) *plano (de la thyoodad)*
What time does the museum open? ¿A qué hora abre el museo? *a ke o-ra a-bre el moo-se-o*	**trip** la excursión *exkoor-syon*
Is the castle open to the public? ¿Está abierto al público el castillo? *esta a-byerto al poo-bleeko el kas-teelyo*	**view** la vista *beesta*
How much does it cost to get in? ¿Cuánto cuesta la entrada? *kwanto kwesta la en-trada*	
Is there a reduction for children/ senior citizens? ¿Hay tarifa reducida para niños/pensionistas? *a-ee ta-reefa redoo-theeda para neenyos/pensyo-neestas*	
Can we take photographs in here? ¿Podemos hacer fotos aquí? *po-demos a-ther fotos a-kee*	
Where can I buy a film? ¿Dónde puedo comprar una película? *don-de pwedo komprar oona pelee-koola*	

Special non-smoking areas in public places are rarer in Spain than in Britain; however, smoking is always forbidden in cinemas, theatres and train compartments.

Do you mind if I smoke? ¿Le importa que fume?
le eem-porta ke foo-me

May I have an ashtray? ¿Me trae un cenicero?
me tra-e oon thenee-thero

Is this a no-smoking area? ¿Está prohibido fumar en esta zona?
esta pro-ee-beedo foomar en es-ta thona

A packet of ... please Un paquete de ..., por favor
oon pa-ke-te de ... por fabor

Have you got any American/English brands? ¿Tiene alguna marca americana/inglesa?
tye-ne al-goona marka a-meree-kana/een-glesa

I'd like some pipe tobacco Querría tabaco de pipa
kerree-a ta-bako de peepa

Do you have any matches/pipe cleaners? ¿Tienen cerillas/escobillas (para limpiar pipas)?
tye-nen the-reelyas/esko-beelyas (para leempyar peepas)

Have you a gas refill for my lighter? ¿Tiene un cargador de gas para mi encendedor?
tye-ne oon karga-dor de gas para mee enthen-dedor

Have you got a light? ¿Tiene fuego?
tye-ne fwego

box of matches
la caja de cerillas
kakha de the-reelyas

cigar
el puro
pooro

cigarette papers
los papeles de fumar
pa-pe-les de foomar

filter-tipped
con filtro
kon feeltro

pipe
la pipa
peepa

without filter
sin filtro
seen feeltro

See also BEACH, ENTERTAINMENT, SAILING, WATERSPORTS, WINTER SPORTS

Which sports activities are available here? ¿Qué actividades deportivas ofrecen aquí?
ke aktee-beeda-des depor-teebas o-fre-then a-kee

Is it possible to go riding/fishing? ¿Se puede montar a caballo/pescar?
se pwe-de montar a ka-balyo/peskar

Where can we play tennis/golf? ¿Dónde podemos jugar al tenis/al golf?
don-de po-demos khoogar al te-nees/al golf

Is there a swimming pool? ¿Hay piscina?
a-ee pees-theena

Are there any interesting walks nearby? ¿Sabe de alguna ruta interesante para pasear por aquí cerca?
sa-be de al-goona roota een-te-re-san-te para pa-se-ar por a-kee therka

Can we rent the equipment? ¿Podemos alquilar el equipo?
po-demos alkee-lar el e-keepo

How much does it cost per hour? ¿A cuánto es la hora?
a kwanto es la o-ra

Do we need to be members? ¿Hace falta ser socio?
a-the falta ser sothyo

Where do we buy our tickets? ¿Dónde podemos sacar los tiquets?
don-de po-demos sakar los tee-ke

Can we take lessons? ¿Dan clases?
dan kla-ses

ball	la bola *bola*
climbing	el alpinismo *alpee-neesmo*
cycling	el ciclismo *thee-kleesmo*
gym shoes	las zapatillas *thapa-teelyas*
gymnasium	el gimnasio *kheem-nasyo*
hill-walking	el montañismo *monta-nyeesmo*
pony-trekking	la excursión a caballo *exkoor-syon a ka-balyo*
racket	la raqueta *ra-keta*
shorts	los pantalones cortos *panta-lo-nes kortos*
squash	el squash *skwosh*
swimming	la natación *nata-thyon*

adhesive tape
la cinta adhesiva
theenta a-de-seeba

biro
el bolígrafo
bolee-grafo

birthday card
la tarjeta de cumpleaños
tar-kheta de koomple-a-nyos

book
el libro
leebro

coloured pencils
los lápices de colores
lapee-thes de kolores

crayons
las ceras de colores
theras de kolo-res

drawing book
el libro de dibujos
leebro de dee-bookhos

envelopes
los sobres
so-bres

felt-tip pen
el rotulador
rotoo-lador

file
la carpeta
kar-peta

glue
la cola
kola

ink
la tinta
teenta

ink cartridge
el cartucho
kar-toocho

luggage tag
la etiqueta
etee-keta

magazine
la revista
re-beesta

newspaper
el periódico
peree-o-deeko

note pad
el bloc
blok

painting book
el libro de pintura
leebro de peen-toora

paints
la caja de pinturas
kakha de peen-tooras

paper
el papel
papel

paperback
el libro de bolsillo
leebro de bol-seelyo

paperclip
el clip
klee

pen
la pluma
plooma

pencil
el lápiz
lapeeth

pencil sharpener
el sacapuntas
saka-poontas

postcard
la (tarjeta) postal
(tar-kheta) postal

refill (for biro)
el recambio
re-kambyo

rubber
la goma de borrar
goma de borrar

stapler
la grapadora
grapa-dora

staples
las grapas
grapas

writing paper
el papel de escribir
papel de eskree-beer

You can either hail a taxi or pick one up at a stand; the driver
will expect a tip of around 10%.

Can you order me a taxi? ¿Puede llamarme un taxi?
pwe-de lyamar-me oon taksee

To the main station/airport please A la estación/al
aeropuerto, por favor
a la esta-thyon/al a-ero-pwerto por fabor

Take me to this address Lléveme a esta dirección
lye-be-me a esta deerek-thyon

Is it far? ¿Está lejos?
esta lekhos

How much will it cost? ¿Cuánto va a costar?
kwanto ba a kostar

I'm in a hurry Tengo prisa
tengo preesa

Can you wait here for a few minutes? ¿Puede esperar aquí
unos minutos?
pwe-de es-perar a-kee oonos mee-nootos

Turn left/right here Tuerza a la izquierda/derecha aquí
twertha a la eeth-kyerda/de-recha a-kee

Please stop here/at the corner Pare aquí/en la esquina, por
favor
pa-re a-kee/en la es-keena por fabor

How much is it? ¿Cuánto es?
kwanto es

It's more than on the meter Eso es más que lo que marca el
contador
eso es mas ke lo ke marka el conta-dor

Keep the change Quédese con el cambio
ke-de-se kon el kambyo

Make it 200 pesetas Cobre 200 pesetas
ko-bre dos-thyentas pe-setas

Can you give me a receipt? ¿Puede darme un recibo?
pwe-de dar-me oon re-theebo

The simplest but most expensive way to phone is from your hotel. You can also go to a *central telefónica*, where you dial the number you want yourself and the clerk will charge you after your call. Pay phones in the streets and in bars require coins.

I want to make a phone call Quiero hacer una llamada telefónica
kyero a-ther oona lya-mada te-lefo-neeka

Can I have a line? ¿Me da linea, por favor?
me da lee-ne-a por fabor

The number is 345 56 78 El número es tres cuatro cinco cinco seis siete ocho
el noo-mero es tres kwatro theenko theenko se-ees sye-te o-cho

I want to reverse the charges Quiero llamar a cobro revertido
kyero lyamar a kobro reber-teedo

Have you got change for the phone? ¿Tiene monedas para el teléfono?
tye-ne mo-nedas para el te-le-fono

What coins do I need? ¿Qué monedas necesito?
ke mo-nedas ne-thesee-to

How much is it to phone England/the USA? ¿Cuánto cuesta llamar por teléfono a Inglaterra/los Estados Unidos?
kwanto kwesta lyamar por te-lefono a eengla-terra/los es-tados oo-needos

I can't get through No contestan
no kon-testan

The line's engaged Está comunicando
esta komoo-neekan-do

crossed line un cruce de linea
kroo-the de lee-ne-a

dialling code el prefijo
pre-feekho

dialling tone el tono de marcar
tono de markar

directory la guia telefónica
gee-a te-le-fonee-ka

extension la extensión
exten-syon

operator el/la telefonista
te-lefo-neesta

phone box la cabina telefónica
ka-beena te-lefo-neeka

receiver el auricular
owree-koolar

transfer charge call la conferencia a cobro revertido
kon-ferenthya a kobro reber-teedo

Hello, this is ... Diga, soy ...
deega soy ...

Can I speak to ...? ¿Se puede poner ...?
se pwe-de po-ner ...

I've been cut off Me han cortado
me an kor-tado

It's a bad line Está mal la línea
esta mal la lee-ne-a

YOU MAY HEAR:

Estoy intentando ponerle
estoy eenten-tando poner-le
I'm trying to connect you

Le pongo
le pongo
I'm putting you through

No cuelgue/Un momento, por favor
no kwel-ge/oon mo-mento por fabor
Hold the line

Lo siento, está comunicando
lo syento esta komoo-neekan-do
I'm sorry, it's engaged

Inténtelo más tarde
eenten-telo mas tar-de
Please try again later

¿De parte de quién?
de par-te de kyen
Who's calling?

Perdone, se ha equivocado de número
perdo-ne se a ekee-boka-do de noo-mero
Sorry, wrong number

See also NUMBERS

What's the time?	**It's:**
¿Qué hora es?	Son:
ke o-ra es	*son*

8.00 las ocho
las o-cho

8.05 las ocho y cinco
las o-cho ee theenko

8.10 las ocho y diez
las o-cho ee dyeth

8.15 las ocho y cuarto
las o-cho ee kwarto

8.20 las ocho y veinte
las o-cho ee be-een-te

8.25 las ocho y veinticinco
las o-cho ee be-eentee-theenko

8.30 las ocho y media
las o-cho ee medya

8.35 las nueve menos veinticinco
las nwe-be menos be-eentee-theenko

8.40 las nueve menos veinte
las nwe-be menos be-een-te

8.45 las nueve menos cuarto
las nwe-be menos kwarto

8.50 las nueve menos diez
las nwe-be menos dyeth

8.55 las nueve menos cinco
las nwe-be menos theenko

12.00 las doce/mediodía   las doce/medianoche
las do-the / medyo-dee-a   *las do-the / medya-no-che*

You may hear the 24-hour clock:

9.00pm 21.00	las veintiuna horas
	las be-eentee-oo-na o-ras
4.45pm 16.45	las catorce horas y cuarenta y cinco minutos
	las kator-the o-ras ee kwa-renta ee theenko
	mee-nootos

What time do you open/close? ¿A qué hora abren/cierran?
*a ke **o**-ra **a**-bren/**thye**rran*

Do we have time to visit the town? ¿Tenemos tiempo para visitar la ciudad?
*te-**nemos tyem**po para beesee-**tar** la thyoo**dad***

How long will it take to get there? ¿Cuánto tardaremos en llegar allí?
kwan**to tarda-**remos** en lye**gar** a-**lyee

We can be there in half an hour Podemos estar allí en media hora
*po-**demos** estar a-**lyee** en **med**ya **o**-ra*

We arrived early/late Llegamos temprano/tarde
*lye-**gamos** tem-**pra**no/**tar**-de*

We should have been there two hours ago Hace dos horas que teníamos que estar allí
*a-the dos **o**-ras ke tenee-**amos** ke estar a-**lyee***

We must be back at the hotel before 11 o'clock Tenemos que volver al hotel antes de las once
*te-**nemos** ke bol-**ber** al o-**tel an**-tes de las **on**-the*

When does the coach leave in the morning? ¿A qué hora sale el autocar por la mañana?
*a ke **o**-ra **sa**-le el owto-**kar** por la ma-**nya**na*

The tour starts at about half past three La excursión empieza sobre las tres y media
*la exkoor-**syon** em-**pye**tha **so**-bre las tres ee **med**ya*

The museum will be open in the morning/afternoon El museo estará abierto por la mañana/por la tarde
*el moo-**se**-o esta-**ra** a-**byer**to por la ma-**nya**na/por la **tar**-de*

The table is booked for 8.30 this evening La mesa está reservada para esta noche a las ocho y media
*la **me**sa esta reser-**ba**da para esta **no**-che a las **o**-cho ee **med**ya*

See also EATING OUT, HOTELS, TAXIS

Tipping is widespread in Spain. Although bills in hotels and restaurants always include service, it is usual to tip waiters (about 10% of the bill), as well as hotel staff. Hairdressers and taxi drivers should also be given about 10%. In bars and cafés it is customary to leave any small change after paying the bill (leave 10-15% if the price list does not say *servicio incluido*). Cinema usherettes and lavatory attendants should receive a few pesetas.

Sorry, I don't have any change Lo siento, no tengo cambio
*lo **syen**to no **ten**go **kam**byo*

Could you give me change of ...? ¿Me puede dar cambio de ...?
*me **pwe**-de dar **kam**byo de ...*

Is it usual to tip ...? ¿Está bien dar ... de propina?
*esta byen dar ... de pro-**pee**na*

How much should I tip? ¿Cuánto tengo que dar de propina?
*kwanto tengo ke dar de pro-**pee**na*

Is the tip included? ¿Está incluida la propina?
*esta eenkloo-**ee**da la pro-**pee**na*

Keep the change Quédese con el cambio
*ke-de-se kon el **kam**byo*

aftershave
el aftershave
after-shave

baby wipes
los pañuelitos
mojados
*panyoo-e-leetos
mo-khados*

cleansing cream
la crema
limpiadora
*krema leempya-
dora*

**contact lens
cleaner**
la solución
limpiadora
*soloo-thyon
leempya-dora*

cotton wool
el algodón
algo-don

deodorant
el desodorante
des-odo-ran-te

emery boards
las limas de uñas
leemas de oo-nyas

eye liner
el rimel
reemel

eye shadow
la sombra de ojos
sombra de o-khos

eyebrow pencil
el lápiz de cujos
lapeeth de kookhos

face cloth
la manopla
ma-nopla

hand cream
la crema de manos
krema de manos

lipstick
la barra de labios
barra de labyos

mascara
el rimel
ree-mel

moisturizer
la leche hidratante
le-che eedra-tan-te

nail file
la lima de uñas
leema de oo-nyas

nail polish
el esmalte para
uñas
*esmal-te para oo-
nyas*

**nail polish
remover**
el quita-esmalte
keeta-esmal-te

nailbrush
el cepillo de uñas
*the-peelyo de oo-
nyas*

perfume
el perfume
perfoo-me

razor
la maquinilla de
afeitar
*makee-neelya de a-
fe-ee-tar*

razor blades
las hojas de afeitar
*o-khas de a-fe-ee-
tar*

shampoo
el champú
champoo

shaving cream
la crema de afeitar
*krema de a-fe-ee-
tar*

soap
el jabón
khabon

sponge
la esponja
espon-kha

sponge bag
la bolsa de aseo
bolsa de a-se-o

sun-tan cream
el aceite
bronceador
*a-the-ee-te bron-
the-a-dor*

talc
los polvos de talco
polbos de talko

tissues
los pañuelos de
papel
*panyoo-e-los de
papel*

toilet water
el agua de colonia
a-gwa de ko-lonya

toothbrush
el cepillo de
dientes
*the-peelyo de
dyen-tes*

toothpaste
la pasta de dientes
pasta de dyen-tes

Public toilets are few and far between, and it's customary to use the toilets in cafés, bars, restaurants and filling stations. It's also customary to tip the attendant, if there is one.

Where is the Gents'/the Ladies'?
¿Dónde están los servicios de caballeros/
de señoras?
*don-de estan los ser-beethyos de kaba-
lyeros/de se-nyoras*

Do you have to pay? ¿Hay que pagar?
a-ee ke pagar

This toilet does not flush Esta cisterna
no funciona
esta thees-terna no foon-thyona

There is no toilet paper/soap No hay
papel higiénico/jabón
no a-ee pa-pel ee-khye-neeko/khabon

**Do I have to pay extra to use the
washbasin?** ¿Tengo que pagar para usar
el lavabo?
tengo ke pagar para oo-sar el la-babo

Is there a toilet for the disabled? ¿Hay
wáter especial para minusválidos?
*a-ee ba-ter es-pethyal para meenoos-
balee-dos*

**Are there facilities for mothers with
babies?** ¿Hay alguna sala para madres
lactantes?
a-ee al-goona sala para ma-dres laktan-tes

The towels have run out Se han acabado
las toallas
se an aka-bado las to-a-lyas

The door will not close No se puede
cerrar la puerta
no se pwe-de the-rrar la pwerta

attendant
el/la empleado/a
em-ple-a-do/a-da

contraceptives
los preservativos
preser-batee-bos

mirror
el espejo
es-pekho

sanitary towels
las compresas
kom-presas

seat
el asiento
a-syento

tampons
los tampones
tampo-nes

**vending
machine**
el distribuidor
automático
*deestree-bweedor
owto-matee-ko*

waste bin
el cubo (de la
basura)
*koobo (de la ba-
soora)*

See also RAILWAY STATION, LUGGAGE

Is this the train for ...? ¿Es éste el tren de ...?
es es-te el tren de ...

Is this seat free? ¿Está libre este asiento?
esta leebre es-te a-syento

I have a seat reservation Tengo reservado un asiento
tengo re-serba-do oon a-syento

Can you help me put my suitcase in the luggage rack? ¿Puede ayudarme a poner la maleta en la rejilla?
pwe-de ayoo-dar-me a po-ner la ma-leta en la re-kheelya

May I open the window? ¿Puedo abrir la ventana?
pwedo a-breer la ben-tana

What time do we get to ...? ¿A qué hora llegamos a ...?
a ke o-ra lye-gamos a ...

Do we stop at ...? ¿Paramos en ...?
pa-ramos en ...

Where do I change for ...? ¿Dónde tengo que hacer transbordo para ...?
don-de tengo ke a-ther trans-bordo para ...

Is there a buffet car/restaurant car? ¿Tiene cafetería/vagón-restaurante este tren?
tye-ne ka-fe-teree-a/bagon-restow-ran-te es-te tren

Please tell me when we get to ... Avíseme cuando llegamos a ..., por favor
a-bee-se-me kwando lye-gamos a ... por fabor

alarm
la alarma
a-larma

compartment
el compartimento
kompar-teemen-to

corridor
el pasillo
pa-seelyo

couchette
la litera
lee-tera

driver
el maquinista
makee-neesta

express
el rápido
ra-peedo

guard
el jefe de tren
khe-fe de tren

sleeping car
el coche-cama
ko-che-kama

stopping train
el tren ómnibus
tren omnee-boos

ticket collector
el revisor
rebee-sor

toilet
el wáter
ba-ter

What's the best way to get to ...? ¿Cuál es la mejor manera de ir a ...?
*kwal es la me**khor** ma-**ne**ra de eer a ...*

How much is it to fly to ...? ¿Cuánto cuesta el billete de avión a ...?
*kwanto **kwes**ta el bee-**lye**-te de a-**byon** a ...*

Are there any special cheap fares? ¿Hay alguna tarifa reducida?
*a-ee al-**goo**na ta-**ree**fa redoo-**thee**da*

What times are the trains/flights? ¿Cuál es el horario de los trenes/de los vuelos?
*kwal es el o-**ra**ryo de los **tre**-nes/de los **bwe**los*

Can I buy the tickets here? ¿Puedo sacar los billetes aquí?
*pwedo sa**kar** los bee-**lye**-tes a-**kee***

Can I change my booking? ¿Puedo cambiar el billete?
*pwedo kam**byar** el bee-**lye**-te*

Can you book me on the London flight? ¿Puede darme un asiento en el vuelo de Londres?
*pwe-de **dar**-me oon a-**syen**to en el **bwe**lo de **lon**-dres*

Can I get back to Manchester tonight? ¿Puedo volver a Manchester esta noche?
*pwedo bol-**ber** a manchester esta **no**-che*

Two second class returns to ... Dos billetes de segunda a ..., de ida y vuelta
*dos bee-**lye**-tes de se-**goon**da a ... de **ee**da ee **bwel**ta*

Can you book me into a hotel? ¿Puede reservarme hotel?
*pwe-de reser-**bar**-me o-**tel***

Do you do bookings for shows/concerts? ¿Se pueden sacar aquí entradas para espectáculos/conciertos?
*se **pwe**-den sakar a-**kee** en-**tra**das para espek-**ta**koo-los/kon-**thyer**tos*

A ticket for tonight's performance please Una entrada para la representación de esta noche, por favor
*oona en-**tra**da para la re-presen-**ta**thyon de esta **no**-che por fa**bor***

See also SIGHTSEEING

Are there any sightseeing tours? ¿Hay
excursiones turísticas?
a-ee exkoor-syo-nes toorees-teekas

When is the bus tour of the town? ¿A
qué hora sale el autobús que hace el
recorrido turístico por la ciudad?
*a ke o-ra sa-le el owto-boos ke a-the el
reko-rreedo toorees-teeko por la thyoodad*

How long does the tour take? ¿Cuánto
tiempo dura la excursión?
kwanto tyempo doora la exkoor-syon

**Are there any boat trips on the
river/lake?** ¿Hay excursiones en barco
por el río/lago?
*a-ee exkoor-syo-nes en barko por el ree-
o/lago*

**Are there any guided tours of the
cathedral?** ¿Hay visitas con guía a la
catedral?
a-ee bee-seetas kon gee-a a la ka-tedral

Is there a reduction for a group? ¿Hay
tarifas reducidas para grupos?
a-ee ta-reefas redoo-theedas para groopos

**Is there a reduction for senior
citizens?** ¿Hay tarifas reducidas para
pensionistas?
*a-ee ta-reefas redoo-theedas para pensyo-
neestas*

Where do we stop for lunch? ¿Dónde
paramos para comer?
don-de pa-ramos para ko-mer

**Please stop the bus, my son/daughter
is feeling sick!** Por favor, pare el
autobús, mi hijo/hija se ha mareado
*por fabor pa-re el owto-boos mee ee-
kho/ee-kha se a ma-re-ado*

coach trip
la excursión en
autocar
*exkoor-syon en
owto-kar*

excursion
la excursión
exkoor-syon

fare
el precio del billete
*prethyo del bee-
lye-te*

organized
organizado
orga-neetha-do

party
el grupo
groopo

ticket
el billete
bee-lye-te

visit
la visita
bee-seeta

zoo
el zoo
tho

bottle opener
el abrebotellas
a-brebo-telyas

broom
la escoba
es-koba

can opener
el abrelatas
a-brela-tas

chair
la silla
seelya

cloth
el trapo
trapo

clothespeg
la pinza
peentha

coat hanger
la percha
percha

comb
el peine
pe-ee-ne

contact lenses
los lentes de
contacto
*len-tes de kon-
takto*

corkscrew
el sacacorchos
saka-korchos

dish
el plato
plato

elastic band
la goma (elástica)
goma (e-lastee-ka)

flask
el frasco
frasko

fork
el tenedor
te-nedor

frying-pan
el sartén
sar-ten

glasses
las gafas
gafas

hairbrush
el cepillo (para el
pelo)
*the-peelyo (para el
pelo)*

hairgrip
la horquilla
or-keelya

handkerchief
el pañuelo
pa-nywelo

knife
el cuchillo
koo-cheelyo

**needle and
thread**
la aguja e hilo
a-gookha e ee-lo

penknife
la navaja
na-bakha

plate
el plato
plato

plug
el enchufe
enchoo-fe

rope
la cuerda
kwerda

safety pin
el imperdible
eem-perdee-ble

saucepan
la cacerola
ka-thero-la

scissors
las tijeras
tee-kheras

spoon
la cuchara
koo-chara

torch
la linterna
leen-terna

umbrella
el paraguas
pa-ragwas

vacuum cleaner
la aspiradora
aspee-rado-ra

**washing-up
liquid**
el (líquido)
lavavajillas
*(lee-keedo) laba-
bakhee-lyas*

See also BEACH, SAILING

Is it possible to go water-skiing/wind-surfing? ¿Se puede hacer esquí acuático/hacer windsurfing?
se pwe-de a-ther eskee a-kwatee-ko/a-ther ween-soorfeen

Can we rent a motor boat? ¿Podemos alquilar una motora?
po-demos alkee-lar oona mo-tora

Can I rent a sailboard? ¿Puedo alquilar una tabla de windsurfing?
pwedo alkee-lar oona tabla de ween-soorfeen

Can one swim in the river? ¿Se puede nadar en el río?
se pwe-de nadar en el ree-o

Can we fish here? ¿Podemos pescar aquí?
po-demos peskar a-kee

Is there a paddling pool for the children? ¿Hay un estanque de juegos para los niños?
a-ee oon estan-ke de khwegos para los neenyos

Do you give lessons? ¿Dan clases?
dan kla-ses

Where is the municipal swimming pool? ¿Dónde está la piscina municipal?
don-de esta la pees-theena moonee-theepal

Is the pool heated? ¿Está climatizada la piscina?
esta kleema-teetha-da la pees-theena

Is it an outdoor pool? ¿Es una piscina al aire libre?
eos oona pees-theena al a-ee-re lee-bre

canoe
la canoa
kano-a

flippers
las aletas
a-letas

goggles
las gafas de bucear
gafas de boo-the-ar

life jacket
el chaleco salvavidas
cha-leko salba-beedas

oar
el remo
remo

rowing boat
la barca
barka

scuba-diving
el submarinismo
soobma-reenees-mo

snorkel
el tubo
toobo

swimsuit
el traje de baño
tra-khe de banyo

wetsuit
el traje de bucear
tra-khe de boo-the-ar

It's a lovely day Hace un día estupendo
a-the oon dee-a estoo-pendo

What dreadful weather! ¡Qué tiempo tan horrible!
ke tyempo tan o-rree-ble

It is raining/snowing Está lloviendo/nevando
esta lyo-byendo/ne-bando

It's windy Hace viento
a-the byento

There's a nice breeze blowing Sopla una brisa muy agradable
sopla oona brisa mooy agra-da-ble

Will it be cold tonight? ¿Hará frío esta noche?
a-ra free-o esta no-che

Is it going to rain/to snow? ¿Va a llover/a nevar?
ba a lyo-ber/a nebar

Will there be a frost? ¿Va a helar?
ba a e-lar

Will there be a thunderstorm? ¿Va a haber tormenta?
ba a a-ber tor-menta

Is it going to be fine? ¿Va a hacer buen tiempo?
ba a a-ther bwen tyempo

Is the weather going to change? ¿Va a cambiar el tiempo?
ba a kambyar el tyempo

What is the temperature? ¿Qué temperatura hace?
ke tem-pera-toora a-the

---

calm
calmo/sin viento
kalmo/seen byento

clouds
las nubes
noo-bes

cool
fresco
fresko

fog
la niebla
nyebla

foggy
nebuloso/de niebla
neboo-loso/de nyebla

hot
(hace) mucho calor
(a-the) moocho kalor

mild
templado
tem-plado

mist
la neblina
ne-bleena

misty
nebuloso
neboo-loso

sunny
(hace) sol
(a-the) sol

warm
(hace) calor
(a-the) kalor

wet
lluvioso
lyoo-byoso

We'd like an aperitif ¿Nos trae un aperitivo?
nos tra-e oon a-peree-teebo

May I have the wine list please? ¿Me trae la carta de vinos, por favor?
me tra-e la karta de beenos por fabor

Can you recommend a good red/white/rosé wine? ¿Puede recomendarnos un tinto/un blanco/un rosado bueno?
pwe-de reko-mendar-nos oon teento/oon blanko/oon ro-sado bweno

A bottle/jug of house wine Una botella/una jarra de vino de la casa
oona bo-telya/oona kharra de beeno de la kasa

A half bottle of ... Media botella de ...
medya bo-telya de ...

Would you bring another glass please? ¿Nos trae otro vaso, por favor?
nos tra-e o-tro baso por fabor

This wine is not chilled Este vino no está fresco
es-te beeno no esta fresko

What liqueurs do you have? ¿Qué licores tienen?
ke leeko-res tye-nen

I'll have a brandy/a Scotch Tráigame un coñac/un whisky
tra-eega-me oon konyak/oon weeskee

A gin and tonic Un gin tonic
oon jeen toneek

A Martini and lemonade Un Martini con gaseosa
oon mar-teenee kon ga-se-o-sa

champagne el champán
champan

dry seco
seko

medium semi-seco
semee-seko

port el oporto
o-porto

sherry el jerez
khe-reth

soda la soda
soda

sparkling espumoso
espoo-moso

sweet dulce
dool-the

vermouth el vermut
bermoot

vodka la vodka
bodka

See also EATING OUT, WINES AND SPIRITS

Albariño del Palacio White wine to be drunk young
Alella Region near Barcelona producing fruity reds/whites
Alicante Region producing strong, full-bodied reds
Castellblanch Fruity, sweet and sparkling wine
Chacolí Sparkling young red/white wines (*Basque Country*)
Champaña Champagne
Fondillón Dark red wine from Alicante
Jerez Sherry; Jerez de la Frontera is the centre of the sherry industry. *Fino* light, dry very pale sherry; *oloroso* cream sherry; *amontillado* medium sherry; *palo cortado* midway between an oloroso and a fino
Jumilla Dry red wines
Lágrima The best Málaga wine
Laguardia Light red wine from the Rioja Alavesa
León Light dry wine from Northern Spain
Málaga Sweet dark dessert wines
Moscatel Sweet wine made from muscat grapes
Navarra Full-bodied ordinary red wines
Penedés Good quality wines and white sparkling wine
Ribeiro Young fresh wine from the Orense region
Rioja Region producing some of Spain's best table wines and subdivided into three areas: *Rioja Alavesa*, *Rioja Alta*, and *Rioja Baja*
Sangría Iced drink with red wine, brandy, lemonade, fruit, ice
San Sadurní de Noya Sparkling white wines
Valdepeñas Lightish red and white wines

Vino blanco/tinto/rosado White/red/rosé wine
Vino común/corriente Ordinary wine
Vino clarete Light red wine
Vino dulce/seco Sweet/dry wine
Vino espumoso Sparkling wine
Vino de la mesa/de la casa Table/house wine
Vino del país Local wine
Vino verde 'Green' wine to be drunk young

Can we hire skis here? ¿Podemos alquilar esquís aquí?
po-demos alkee-lar eskees a-kee

Could you adjust my bindings? ¿Me puede ajustar las fijaciones?
me pwe-de akhoos-tar las feekha-thyo-nes

A 3-day ticket please Un forfait de tres días, por favor
oon for-fa-ee de tres dee-as por fabor

What are the snow conditions? ¿Cuál es el estado de la nieve?
kwal es el es-tado de la nye-be

Is there a restaurant at the top station? ¿Hay restaurante en la cota alta?
a-ee restow-ran-te en la kota alta

Which are the easiest runs? ¿Cuáles son las pistas más fáciles?
kwa-les son las peestas mas fathee-les

We'll take the gondola Cogeremos el telecabina
ko-khe-remos el te-leka-beena

When is the last ascent? ¿A qué hora es la última súbida?
a ke o-ra es la ool-teema soo-beeda

Is there danger of avalanches? ¿Hay peligro de aludes?
a-ee pelee-gro de a-loo-des

The snow is very icy/heavy La nieve está muy helada/dura
la nye-be esta mooy e-lada/doora

Where can we go skating? ¿Dónde podemos ir a patinar sobre hielo?
don-de po-demos eer a patee-nar so-bre yelo

Is there a toboggan run? ¿Hay una pista para trineos?
a-ee oona peesta para tree-ne-os

cablecar
el teleférico
te-le-fe-reeko

chairlift
el telesilla
te-le-seelya

goggles
las gafas de esquí
gafas de eskee

instructor
el instructor
eenstrook-tor

lift pass
el forfait
for-fa-ee

rink
la pista de patinaje
peesta de patee-na-khe

skates
los patines
patee-nes

ski boot
la bota de esquí
bota de eskee

ski pole
el palo de esquí
palo de eskee

ski suit
el traje de esquí
tra-khe de eskee

The following is a list of all the key words used in this book,
with a cross reference to the topic(s) under which they appear.
If you don't find the word you are looking for in the wordlist on
any given page — look through the phrases.

aboard → SAILING
accelerator → CAR PARTS
accident → ACCIDENTS
activities → SPORTS
address → PERSONAL DETAILS
adhesive tape → REPAIRS,
  STATIONERY
admission charge
  → ENTERTAINMENT
adult → FERRIES
advance, in a. → LUGGAGE,
  PAYING
afternoon → TIME PHRASES
aftershave → TOILETRIES
air line → PETROL STATION
air mail → POST OFFICE
air-mattress → CAMPING AND
  CARAVANNING
airport → AIRPORT
alarm → TRAIN TRAVEL
alcohol → CUSTOMS AND
  PASSPORTS
allowance → CUSTOMS AND
  PASSPORTS
altar → CHURCH AND WORSHIP
alternator → CAR PARTS
ambulance → ACCIDENTS –
  INJURIES, EMERGENCIES
America → POST OFFICE
American → SMOKING
anchor, to → SAILING
ankle → BODY
antiseptic → CHEMIST'S
apartment → SELF-CATERING

aperitif → WINES AND SPIRITS
apples → FOOD – FRUIT AND VEG
appointment → BUSINESS,
  DOCTOR, HAIRDRESSER'S
arm → BODY
armbands → BEACH
arrival → RAILWAY STATION
arrive, to → COACH TRAVEL
ashtray → SMOKING
asparagus → FOOD – FRUIT AND
  VEG
aspirin → CHEMIST'S
attendant → PETROL STATION,
  TOILETS
aubergine → FOOD – FRUIT AND
  VEG
automatic → CAR PARTS
avalanche → WINTER SPORTS
avocado → FOOD – FRUIT AND
  VEG
avoid, to → ROAD CONDITIONS
baby → CHILDREN
baby food → CHILDREN
baby wipes → TOILETRIES
babysitter → CHILDREN
babysitting service → CHILDREN
back → BODY
bag → LUGGAGE
baggage reclaim → AIRPORT
balcony → ACCOMMODATION
ball → SPORTS
bananas → FOOD – FRUIT AND
  VEG

bandage → ACCIDENTS –
  INJURIES, CHEMIST'S
bank → MONEY
baptism → CELEBRATIONS
bar → ENTERTAINMENT, HOTEL
  DESK
bathroom → ACCOMMODATION
battery → CAR PARTS
beach → BEACH
beautiful → DESCRIBING THINGS
bed → DOCTOR
bedding → SELF-CATERING
bedroom → SELF-CATERING
beef → FOOD – GENERAL
beer → DRINKS
beetroot → FOOD – FRUIT AND
  VEG
begin, to → NIGHTLIFE
beige → COLOURS AND SHAPES
belt → CLOTHES
best wishes → CELEBRATIONS
big → CLOTHES, COLOURS AND
  SHAPES
bigger → BUYING
bill → EATING OUT, ORDERING,
  PAYING, ROOM SERVICE
biro → STATIONERY
birthday → CELEBRATIONS
birthday card → STATIONERY
bit, a b. → DENTIST
bitten → DOCTOR
bitter → DESCRIBING THINGS
black → COLOURS AND SHAPES,
  PHOTOGRAPHY
black coffee → DRINKS
black ice → ROAD CONDITIONS
blanket → ROOM SERVICE
bleeding → ACCIDENTS –
  INJURIES, DENTIST

blind → PERSONAL DETAILS
blood → CLEANING
blood group → PERSONAL
  DETAILS
blood pressure → DOCTOR
blouse → CLOTHES
blow-dry → HAIRDRESSER'S
blue → COLOURS AND SHAPES
boat → BEACH
boat trip → TRIPS AND
  EXCURSIONS
body → BODY
bone → BODY
bonnet → CAR PARTS
book → STATIONERY
book of tickets → CITY TRAVEL
book, to → ENTERTAINMENT,
  TRAVEL AGENT
booking → HOTEL DESK, TRAVEL
  AGENT
booking office
  → ENTERTAINMENT
boot → CAR PARTS
bottle → CHILDREN, WINES AND
  SPIRITS
bottle opener → USEFUL ITEMS
bow → SAILING
box of matches → SMOKING
boy → CHILDREN
bra → CLOTHES
bracelet → GIFTS AND
  SOUVENIRS
brake fluid → CAR PARTS
brakes → CAR PARTS
brand → SMOKING
brandy → WINES AND SPIRITS
bread → EATING OUT, FOOD –
  GENERAL
breakdown van → BREAKDOWNS

breakfast → ACCOMMODATION, ROOM SERVICE
breast → BODY
breathe, to → ACCIDENTS – INJURIES
breeze → WEATHER
bring, to → WINES AND SPIRITS
Britain → PERSONAL DETAILS
British → CUSTOMS AND PASSPORTS, PROBLEMS
broken → COMPLAINTS, REPAIRS
broken down → BREAKDOWNS
brooch → GIFTS AND SOUVENIRS
broom → USEFUL ITEMS
brown → COLOURS AND SHAPES
bucket → BEACH
buffet → RAILWAY STATION
buffet car → TRAIN TRAVEL
bulb → BREAKDOWNS
bureau de change → MONEY
bus → AIRPORT, CITY TRAVEL, COACH TRAVEL, TRIPS AND EXCURSIONS
bus depot → COACH TRAVEL
bus stop → CITY TRAVEL
bus tour → TRIPS AND EXCURSIONS
business → CUSTOMS AND PASSPORTS, PERSONAL DETAILS
business card → BUSINESS
butter → FOOD – GENERAL
buttocks → BODY
button → CLOTHES, REPAIRS
buy, to → GIFTS AND SOUVENIRS
cabaret → NIGHTLIFE
cabin → FERRIES
cablecar → WINTER SPORTS
café → EATING OUT

calm → WEATHER
camera → PHOTOGRAPHY
camp, to → CAMPING AND CARAVANNING
camp-bed → CAMPING AND CARAVANNING
campsite → CAMPING AND CARAVANNING
can → PETROL STATION
can opener → USEFUL ITEMS
canoe → WATERSPORTS
captain → FERRIES
car → ACCIDENTS – CARS, AIRPORT, BREAKDOWNS, CAR HIRE
car documents → CAR HIRE
car number → POLICE
car park → DRIVING ABROAD
car wash → PETROL STATION
caravan → CAMPING AND CARAVANNING
carburettor → CAR PARTS
cardigan → CLOTHES
carrier bag → SHOPPING
carrots → FOOD – FRUIT AND VEG
cartridge → PHOTOGRAPHY
case → LUGGAGE
cash → MONEY, PAYING
cash advance → MONEY
cash desk → PAYING, SHOPPING
cash, to → MONEY
cashier → PAYING
casino → NIGHTLIFE
cassette → PHOTOGRAPHY
castle → SIGHTSEEING
catalogue → BUSINESS
catch, to → COACH TRAVEL

cathedral → CHURCH AND WORSHIP, SIGHTSEEING
Catholic → CHURCH AND WORSHIP
cauliflower → FOOD – FRUIT AND VEG
celery → FOOD – FRUIT AND VEG
chains → ROAD CONDITIONS
chair → USEFUL ITEMS
chairlift → WINTER SPORTS
champagne → WINES AND SPIRITS
change → BUYING, MONEY, TAXIS, TELEPHONE
change, to → AIRPORT, BEACH, CHILDREN, CITY TRAVEL, RAILWAY STATION, WEATHER
changing room → SHOPPING
Channel, the → FERRIES
chapel → CHURCH AND WORSHIP
charge → PAYING
chauffeur → CAR HIRE
cheap → TRAVEL AGENT
cheaper → BUYING, PAYING
check in, to → AIRPORT, LUGGAGE
check, to → PETROL STATION
check-in desk → AIRPORT
cheek → BODY
cheers! → CELEBRATIONS
cheese → EATING OUT, FOOD – GENERAL
chemist's → ASKING QUESTIONS
cheque → PAYING
cheque book → MONEY
cheque card → PAYING
cherries → FOOD – FRUIT AND VEG
chest → BODY

chicken → FOOD – GENERAL
children → CHILDREN
chilled → WINES AND SPIRITS
chocolates → GIFTS AND SOUVENIRS
choke → CAR PARTS
christening → CELEBRATIONS
Christmas → CELEBRATIONS
church → CHURCH AND WORSHIP
churchyard → CHURCH AND WORSHIP
cigar → SMOKING
cigarette papers → SMOKING
cigarettes → BUYING
cine-camera → PHOTOGRAPHY
cinema → ENTERTAINMENT
circular → COLOURS AND SHAPES
city → MAPS AND GUIDES
clean → DESCRIBING THINGS
clean, to → CLEANING, PETROL STATION
cleaner → SELF-CATERING
cleansing cream → TOILETRIES
clear → ROAD CONDITIONS
clerk → POST OFFICE
climbing → SPORTS
close → ACCIDENTS – CARS
close, to → SHOPPING, TIME PHRASES
closed → SHOPPING
cloth → USEFUL ITEMS
clothes → CLOTHES
clothespeg → USEFUL ITEMS
clouds → WEATHER
club → ENTERTAINMENT
clutch → CAR PARTS
coach trip → TRIPS AND EXCURSIONS

dry cleaner's → CLEANING
dry, to → CLEANING
dummy → CHILDREN
duty-free → FERRIES
duty-free shop → AIRPORT
dynamo → CAR PARTS
ear → BODY
earache → DOCTOR
earrings → GIFTS AND
  SOUVENIRS
easy → DESCRIBING THINGS
eat, to → ORDERING
eggs → FOOD – GENERAL
elastic band → USEFUL ITEMS
elbow → BODY
electric razor → ROOM SERVICE
electricity → CAMPING AND
  CARAVANNING
electrics → BREAKDOWNS
embassy → EMERGENCIES
emergency windscreen
  → BREAKDOWNS
emery boards → TOILETRIES
engaged → TELEPHONE
engine → CAR PARTS, SAILING
England → CONVERSATION –
  GENERAL, POST OFFICE
English → PERSONAL DETAILS,
  PROBLEMS
enjoy, to → CELEBRATIONS
enough → MEASUREMENTS,
  MONEY, PAYING
entry visa → CUSTOMS AND
  PASSPORTS
envelopes → STATIONERY
equipment → SPORTS
escalator → CITY TRAVEL
Eurocheque → MONEY
evening → NIGHTLIFE

evening meal
  → ACCOMMODATION
excellent → DESCRIBING THINGS
excess luggage → LUGGAGE
exchange rate → MONEY
excursion → TRIPS AND
  EXCURSIONS
exhaust pipe → CAR PARTS
exhibition → BUSINESS
exit → SHOPPING
expect, to → BUSINESS
expensive → BUYING, PAYING
exposure meter
  → PHOTOGRAPHY
express → POST OFFICE, TRAIN
  TRAVEL
extension → TELEPHONE
extra → HOTEL DESK
eye → BODY
eye liner → TOILETRIES
eye shadow → TOILETRIES
eyebrow pencil → TOILETRIES
fabric → CLOTHES
face → BODY
face cloth → TOILETRIES
facilities → CHILDREN
factory → PERSONAL DETAILS
faint, to → DOCTOR
fall → ACCIDENTS – INJURIES
fan belt → CAR PARTS
far → DESCRIBING THINGS,
  DIRECTIONS
fare → CITY TRAVEL, TRAVEL
  AGENT, TRIPS AND EXCURSIONS
fast → ACCIDENTS – CARS,
  DESCRIBING THINGS
fat → COLOURS AND SHAPES
feed, to → CHILDREN
felt-tip pen → STATIONERY

festival → CELEBRATIONS
fetch, to → EMERGENCIES
file → STATIONERY
fill up, to → PETROL STATION
filling → DENTIST
film → NIGHTLIFE, PHOTOGRAPHY
film show → COACH TRAVEL
filter → SMOKING
filter-tipped → SMOKING
fine → GREETINGS, POLICE, WEATHER
finger → BODY
fire → EMERGENCIES
fire brigade → EMERGENCIES
first class → RAILWAY STATION
fish → FOOD – GENERAL
fish, to → WATERSPORTS
fishing → SPORTS
flash → PHOTOGRAPHY
flash bulb → PHOTOGRAPHY
flash cube → PHOTOGRAPHY
flask → USEFUL ITEMS
flat tyre → BREAKDOWNS
flaw → COMPLAINTS
flight → AIRPORT
flight bag → LUGGAGE
flippers → WATERSPORTS
flour → FOOD – GENERAL
flowers → GIFTS AND SOUVENIRS
flush, to → TOILETS
fly sheet → CAMPING AND CARAVANNING
fly, to → TRAVEL AGENT
fog → ROAD CONDITIONS, WEATHER
foggy → WEATHER
food poisoning → DOCTOR
foot → BODY

forget, to → EMERGENCIES
forgotten → PROBLEMS
fork → USEFUL ITEMS
form → POST OFFICE
free → TRAIN TRAVEL
French beans → FOOD – FRUIT AND VEG
frequent → CITY TRAVEL
fridge → SELF-CATERING
fringe → HAIRDRESSER'S
frost → ROAD CONDITIONS, WEATHER
fruit juice → DRINKS
frying-pan → USEFUL ITEMS
full board → BOOKING ACCOMMODATION
fun fair → ENTERTAINMENT
fur → CLOTHES
fuse → CAR PARTS, SELF-CATERING
garage → BREAKDOWNS, PETROL STATION
garlic → FOOD – FRUIT AND VEG
gas → SELF-CATERING
gas cylinder → CAMPING AND CARAVANNING
gas refill → SMOKING
gears → CAR PARTS
Gents' → TOILETS
get in, to → NIGHTLIFE, SIGHTSEEING
get off, to → CITY TRAVEL, COACH TRAVEL
get through, to → TELEPHONE
gift → SHOPPING
gift shop → GIFTS AND SOUVENIRS
gin → WINES AND SPIRITS
girl → CHILDREN

Giro account → POST OFFICE
glass → DRINKS, WINES AND SPIRITS
glasses → USEFUL ITEMS
gloves → CLOTHES
glue → REPAIRS
goggles → WATERSPORTS
gold → COLOURS AND SHAPES
golf → SPORTS
good → ASKING QUESTIONS, DESCRIBING THINGS
good afternoon → GREETINGS
good evening → GREETINGS
good morning → GREETINGS
good night → GREETINGS
goodbye → GREETINGS
gown → HAIRDRESSER'S
gramme → BUYING, MEASUREMENTS
grapefruit → FOOD – FRUIT AND VEG
grapes → FOOD – FRUIT AND VEG
green → COLOURS AND SHAPES
green card → ACCIDENTS – CARS, POLICE
grey → COLOURS AND SHAPES
group → TRIPS AND EXCURSIONS
guard → RAILWAY STATION, TRAIN TRAVEL
guide book → MAPS AND GUIDES, SIGHTSEEING
guided tour → SIGHTSEEING, TRIPS AND EXCURSIONS
gums → DENTIST
guy rope → CAMPING AND CARAVANNING
gym shoes → SPORTS
gymnasium → SPORTS
hair → HAIRDRESSER'S

hair spray → HAIRDRESSER'S
hairbrush → USEFUL ITEMS
hairdryer → ROOM SERVICE
hairgrip → USEFUL ITEMS
half bottle → WINES AND SPIRITS
half fare → CITY TRAVEL
half-board → ACCOMMODATION
ham → FOOD – GENERAL
hammer → REPAIRS
hand → BODY
hand cream → TOILETRIES
hand luggage → LUGGAGE
hand-made → GIFTS AND SOUVENIRS
handbag → EMERGENCIES
handbrake → CAR PARTS
handkerchief → USEFUL ITEMS
handle → REPAIRS
harbour → SAILING
hard → DESCRIBING THINGS
hat → CLOTHES
hay fever → DOCTOR
hazard lights → BREAKDOWNS
head → BODY
headache → CHEMIST'S, DOCTOR
headlights → CAR PARTS
heart → BODY
heating → SELF-CATERING
heavy → DESCRIBING THINGS, LUGGAGE
heavy rain → ROAD CONDITIONS
hello → GREETINGS
help → EMERGENCIES
help, to → ASKING QUESTIONS, PROBLEMS
high chair → CHILDREN
high tide → BEACH
hill-walking → SPORTS

last, to → NIGHTLIFE
late → HOTEL DESK
later → TELEPHONE
launderette → CLEANING
laundry room → CLEANING
laundry service → CLEANING
lavatory → PETROL STATION
law → ACCIDENTS – CARS
lawyer → ACCIDENTS – CARS,
  POLICE
laxative → CHEMIST'S
layered → HAIRDRESSER'S
leak → BREAKDOWNS
leather → CLOTHES
leave, to → COACH TRAVEL,
  TIME PHRASES
leeks → FOOD – FRUIT AND VEG
left → DIRECTIONS
left luggage → LUGGAGE,
  RAILWAY STATION
leg → BODY
lemon → COLOURS AND SHAPES,
  FOOD – FRUIT AND VEG
lemon tea → DRINKS
lemonade → DRINKS
lens → PHOTOGRAPHY
lens cover → PHOTOGRAPHY
less → MEASUREMENTS
lessons → SPORTS
let off, to → COACH TRAVEL
letter → POST OFFICE
lettuce → FOOD – FRUIT AND
  VEG
life jacket → FERRIES,
  WATERSPORTS
lifeboat → FERRIES
lifeguard → BEACH
lift → ACCOMMODATION

light → CLOTHES, COLOURS AND
  SHAPES, DESCRIBING THINGS,
  SELF-CATERING, SMOKING
lighter → SMOKING
like, to → CONVERSATION –
  GENERAL
line → TELEPHONE
lipstick → TOILETRIES
liqueur → WINES AND SPIRITS
literature → BUSINESS
litre → FOOD – GENERAL,
  MEASUREMENTS, PETROL
  STATION
live, to → PERSONAL DETAILS
liver → BODY, FOOD – GENERAL
living room → SELF-CATERING
local → MAPS AND GUIDES,
  ORDERING
lock → COMPLAINTS
locked out → ROOM SERVICE
locker → LUGGAGE
long → COLOURS AND SHAPES,
  DESCRIBING THINGS,
  HAIRDRESSER'S
look for, to → SHOPPING
lost → DIRECTIONS
lost property office
  → EMERGENCIES
lounge → AIRPORT, HOTEL DESK
lovely → DESCRIBING THINGS,
  WEATHER
low tide → BEACH
luggage → LUGGAGE
luggage allowance → LUGGAGE
luggage hold → COACH TRAVEL
luggage rack → LUGGAGE
luggage tag → STATIONERY
luggage trolley → LUGGAGE
lung → BODY

magazine → STATIONERY
main → SHOPPING
main course → EATING OUT
major road → DRIVING ABROAD
mallet → CAMPING AND
   CARAVANNING
manage, to → LUGGAGE
manager → HOTEL DESK
map → MAPS AND GUIDES
margarine → FOOD – GENERAL
market → SHOPPING
Martini → WINES AND SPIRITS
mascara → TOILETRIES
mass → CHURCH AND WORSHIP
mast → SAILING
matches → SMOKING
material → CLOTHES
mauve → COLOURS AND SHAPES
meal → ORDERING
measure, to → CLOTHES
mechanic → BREAKDOWNS
medicine → DOCTOR
medium → WINES AND SPIRITS
medium rare → ORDERING
melon → FOOD – FRUIT AND VEG
member → NIGHTLIFE
menu → EATING OUT, ORDERING
message → BUSINESS
meter → SELF-CATERING, TAXIS
metre → SHOPPING
mild → WEATHER
milk → DRINKS, FOOD –
   GENERAL
mince → FOOD – GENERAL
mind, to → SMOKING
mineral water → DRINKS
minister → CHURCH AND
   WORSHIP
minor road → DRIVING ABROAD

minute → TIME
mirror → TOILETS
missing → EMERGENCIES
mist → WEATHER
misty → WEATHER
moisturizer → TOILETRIES
money → MONEY
money order → POST OFFICE
more → MEASUREMENTS
morning → TIME PHRASES
mosque → CHURCH AND
   WORSHIP
mother → TOILETS
motor boat → WATERSPORTS
motorway → DRIVING ABROAD
mouth → BODY
move, to → ACCIDENTS –
   INJURIES
movie camera → PHOTOGRAPHY
municipal → WATERSPORTS
muscle → BODY
museum → SIGHTSEEING
mushrooms → FOOD – FRUIT
   AND VEG
mustard → FOOD – GENERAL
nail → REPAIRS
nail file → TOILETRIES
nail polish → TOILETRIES
nail polish remover
   → TOILETRIES
nailbrush → TOILETRIES
name → PERSONAL DETAILS
nappy → CHILDREN
national → CUSTOMS AND
   PASSPORTS
near → DESCRIBING THINGS,
   DIRECTIONS
nearest → DIRECTIONS
neck → BODY

necklace → GIFTS AND SOUVENIRS
need, to → DOCTOR
needle and thread → USEFUL ITEMS
negative → PHOTOGRAPHY
new → DESCRIBING THINGS
New Year → CELEBRATIONS
newspaper → STATIONERY
next → FERRIES, RAILWAY STATION
nice → WEATHER
night → HOTEL DESK
night club → NIGHTLIFE
nightdress → CLOTHES
no → CONVERSATION – MEETING
noisy → COMPLAINTS
non-smoking → AIRPORT
nose → BODY
note → MONEY
note pad → STATIONERY
number → PERSONAL DETAILS
nylon → CLOTHES
oar → WATERSPORTS
oblong → COLOURS AND SHAPES
offence → ACCIDENTS – CARS
office → PERSONAL DETAILS
oil → FOOD – GENERAL, PETROL STATION
old → DESCRIBING THINGS
olives → FOOD – FRUIT AND VEG
one-way → DRIVING ABROAD
onions → FOOD – FRUIT AND VEG
open → SHOPPING
open, to → SIGHTSEEING, TIME PHRASES
operate, to → CAR HIRE
operation → DOCTOR

operator → TELEPHONE
orange → COLOURS AND SHAPES
oranges → FOOD – FRUIT AND VEG
orchestra → ENTERTAINMENT
order → ORDERING
organized → TRIPS AND EXCURSIONS
ornament → GIFTS AND SOUVENIRS
outside line → ROOM SERVICE
oval → COLOURS AND SHAPES
over → DIRECTIONS
over there → DIRECTIONS
overheat, to → BREAKDOWNS
packet → SMOKING
paddling pool → WATERSPORTS
pain → DOCTOR
painful → DOCTOR
painting book → STATIONERY
paints → STATIONERY
panties → CLOTHES
pants → CLOTHES
paper → STATIONERY
paper bag → SHOPPING
paperback → STATIONERY
paperclip → STATIONERY
parcel → POST OFFICE
park → SIGHTSEEING
park, to → DRIVING ABROAD
parking disc → DRIVING ABROAD
parking meter → DRIVING ABROAD
parking ticket → DRIVING ABROAD
parting → HAIRDRESSER'S
parts → BREAKDOWNS
party → TRIPS AND EXCURSIONS
pass → ROAD CONDITIONS

passport → EMERGENCIES, PERSONAL DETAILS
passport control → AIRPORT
pay, to → PAYING
payment → PAYING
peaches → FOOD – FRUIT AND VEG
pears → FOOD – FRUIT AND VEG
peas → FOOD – FRUIT AND VEG
pen → STATIONERY
pencil → STATIONERY
pencil sharpener → STATIONERY
penicillin → DOCTOR
penknife → USEFUL ITEMS
pepper → FOOD – FRUIT AND VEG, FOOD – GENERAL
per → CAMPING AND CARAVANNING
performance → NIGHTLIFE
perfume → TOILETRIES
perm → HAIRDRESSER'S
peseta → MONEY
petrol → BREAKDOWNS, PETROL STATION
petrol pump → PETROL STATION
petrol station → PETROL STATION
petrol tank → BREAKDOWNS
petticoat → CLOTHES
phone → TELEPHONE
phone box → TELEPHONE
phone call → TELEPHONE
phone, to → TELEPHONE
photocopying → BUSINESS
photos → PHOTOGRAPHY
pill → DOCTOR
pin → REPAIRS
pineapple → FOOD – FRUIT AND VEG

pink → COLOURS AND SHAPES
pint → MEASUREMENTS
pipe → SMOKING
pipe cleaners → SMOKING
pipe tobacco → SMOKING
plane → AIRPORT
plate → USEFUL ITEMS
platform → RAILWAY STATION
play → ENTERTAINMENT
play, to → ENTERTAINMENT, SPORTS
playroom → CHILDREN
pleasant → DESCRIBING THINGS
plug → USEFUL ITEMS
plums → FOOD – FRUIT AND VEG
pointed → COLOURS AND SHAPES
points → CAR PARTS
poisoning → DOCTOR
police → ACCIDENTS – CARS, POLICE
police car → POLICE
police station → POLICE
policeman → POLICE
polyester → CLOTHES
pony-trekking → SPORTS
pork → FOOD – GENERAL
port → WINES AND SPIRITS
porter → HOTEL DESK, LUGGAGE
portion → MEASUREMENTS
possible → SPORTS
post office → POST OFFICE
postage → POST OFFICE
postcard → STATIONERY
pot → DRINKS
potatoes → FOOD – FRUIT AND VEG
pottery → GIFTS AND SOUVENIRS
pound → FOOD – GENERAL, MEASUREMENTS

road map → MAPS AND GUIDES
road sign → DIRECTIONS
road works → ROAD CONDITIONS
rob, to → POLICE
room → HOTEL DESK
room service → HOTEL DESK
rope → USEFUL ITEMS
rosé → WINES AND SPIRITS
rough → DESCRIBING THINGS, FERRIES
round → COLOURS AND SHAPES
route → ROAD CONDITIONS
rowing boat → WATERSPORTS
rubber → STATIONERY
rudder → SAILING
run out, to → BREAKDOWNS, PROBLEMS
safe → BEACH, CHEMIST'S
safety pin → REPAIRS, USEFUL ITEMS
sail → SAILING
sailboard → WATERSPORTS
sailing → FERRIES
salt → FOOD – GENERAL
sample → BUSINESS
sandals → CLOTHES
sandwich → EATING OUT
sanitary towels → CHEMIST'S
saucepan → USEFUL ITEMS
scarf → CLOTHES
scissors → USEFUL ITEMS
Scotch → WINES AND SPIRITS
Scottish → PERSONAL DETAILS
screw → REPAIRS
screwdriver → REPAIRS
scuba-diving → WATERSPORTS
sea → BEACH, FERRIES
seasick → SAILING
season ticket → CITY TRAVEL

seat → COACH TRAVEL, TOILETS, TRAIN TRAVEL
seat belt → DRIVING ABROAD
seat reservation → TRAIN TRAVEL
second class → RAILWAY STATION, TRAVEL AGENT
secretary → BUSINESS
see, to → SIGHTSEEING
sell, to → BUYING
send, to → POST OFFICE
senior citizen → SIGHTSEEING
serious → ACCIDENTS – INJURIES
serve, to → ORDERING
served, to be → COMPLAINTS
service → CHURCH AND WORSHIP, ORDERING
set → HAIRDRESSER'S
set menu → EATING OUT
shade → COLOURS AND SHAPES
shampoo → TOILETRIES
shandy → DRINKS
shaving cream → TOILETRIES
sheet → SELF-CATERING
sherry → WINES AND SPIRITS
shiny → COLOURS AND SHAPES
ship → FERRIES
shirt → CLOTHES
shock absorber → CAR PARTS
shoes → CLOTHES
shop → BUYING
shopping area → SHOPPING
shopping bag → SHOPPING
short → DESCRIBING THINGS, HAIRDRESSER'S
short cut → DRIVING ABROAD
shorts → CLOTHES, SPORTS
shoulder → BODY
show → NIGHTLIFE

show, to → DIRECTIONS, MAPS
  AND GUIDES
shower → SELF-CATERING
shutter → PHOTOGRAPHY
sick → DOCTOR, TRIPS AND
  EXCURSIONS
sign → DRIVING ABROAD
signature → PAYING
silk → CLOTHES
silver → COLOURS AND SHAPES
single → RAILWAY STATION
single bed → ACCOMMODATION
single room
  → ACCOMMODATION
sink → CLEANING
sit, to → CONVERSATION –
  MEETING
site → CAMPING AND
  CARAVANNING
skates → WINTER SPORTS
skating → WINTER SPORTS
ski boot → WINTER SPORTS
ski pole → WINTER SPORTS
skin → BODY
skirt → CLOTHES
skis → WINTER SPORTS
sleep, to → DOCTOR
sleeper → RAILWAY STATION
sleeping bag → CAMPING AND
  CARAVANNING
sleeping car → TRAIN TRAVEL
slice → MEASUREMENTS
slides → PHOTOGRAPHY
slip, to → ACCIDENTS – INJURIES
slow → DESCRIBING THINGS
small → COLOURS AND SHAPES
smaller → BUYING
smoke, to → SMOKING

smooth → DESCRIBING THINGS,
  FERRIES
snack bar → AIRPORT
snorkel → WATERSPORTS
snow → WINTER SPORTS
snow, to → WEATHER
snowed up → ROAD CONDITIONS
soap → TOILETRIES
socket → ROOM SERVICE
socks → CLOTHES
soft → DESCRIBING THINGS
soft drink → DRINKS
son → PERSONAL DETAILS
sore → CHEMIST'S, DENTIST,
  DOCTOR
sorry → CONVERSATION –
  GENERAL
soup → EATING OUT, FOOD –
  GENERAL
sour → DESCRIBING THINGS
souvenir → GIFTS AND
  SOUVENIRS
spade → BEACH
Spain → CONVERSATION –
  GENERAL
Spanish → CONVERSATION –
  MEETING
spanner → BREAKDOWNS
spare → SELF-CATERING
spark plugs → CAR PARTS
sparkling → WINES AND SPIRITS
speak, to → CONVERSATION –
  MEETING, PROBLEMS,
  TELEPHONE
special → TRAVEL AGENT
special menu → CHILDREN
special rate → CHILDREN
speciality → ORDERING
speed limit → DRIVING ABROAD

spicy → DESCRIBING THINGS
spinach → FOOD – FRUIT AND VEG
spirits → CUSTOMS AND PASSPORTS
sponge → TOILETRIES
sponge bag → TOILETRIES
spoon → USEFUL ITEMS
sports → SPORTS
sprain → ACCIDENTS – INJURIES
square → COLOURS AND SHAPES
squash → SPORTS
stain → CLEANING
stall → SHOPPING
stamps → POST OFFICE
stapler → STATIONERY
staples → STATIONERY
starter → EATING OUT
station → TAXIS
stay → HOTEL DESK
stay, to → CUSTOMS AND PASSPORTS, DOCTOR
steak → FOOD – GENERAL
steering → CAR PARTS
steering wheel → CAR PARTS
sterling → MONEY
stern → SAILING
sticking plaster → CHEMIST'S
stitching → REPAIRS
stockings → CLOTHES
stolen → EMERGENCIES
stomach → BODY
stomach upset → DOCTOR
stop, to → TAXIS, TRAIN TRAVEL, TRIPS AND EXCURSIONS
stopping train → TRAIN TRAVEL
straight → HAIRDRESSER'S
straight on → DIRECTIONS

strawberries → FOOD – FRUIT AND VEG
streaks → HAIRDRESSER'S
street map → MAPS AND GUIDES
street plan → SIGHTSEEING
string → REPAIRS
strong → DESCRIBING THINGS
student → PERSONAL DETAILS
stung → ACCIDENTS – INJURIES
styling mousse → HAIRDRESSER'S
suede → CLOTHES
sugar → FOOD – GENERAL
suit (man's) → CLOTHES
suit (woman's) → CLOTHES
suitable → SHOPPING
suitcase → LUGGAGE
sun-tan cream → TOILETRIES
sunburn → ACCIDENTS – INJURIES
sunglasses → BEACH
sunny → WEATHER
sunshade → BEACH
sunstroke → ACCIDENTS – INJURIES
suntan oil → BEACH
supermarket → BUYING
supplement → RAILWAY STATION
swallow, to → DOCTOR
sweater → CLOTHES
sweet → DESCRIBING THINGS, WINES AND SPIRITS
swim, to → BEACH
swimming → SPORTS
swimming pool → SPORTS
swimsuit → BEACH, CLOTHES
synagogue → CHURCH AND WORSHIP

t-shirt → CLOTHES
table → EATING OUT, ORDERING
table linen → GIFTS AND
  SOUVENIRS
tablet → DOCTOR
tailback → ROAD CONDITIONS
take out, to → DENTIST
take up, to → HOTEL DESK
take, to → CHEMIST'S,
  DIRECTIONS, SPORTS
talc → TOILETRIES
tampons → CHEMIST'S
tap → CLEANING
tape → REPAIRS
tax → PAYING
taxi → TAXIS
tea → DRINKS, FOOD – GENERAL
telegram → POST OFFICE
telephone → PETROL STATION
telex → BUSINESS
tell, to → TRAIN TRAVEL
temperature → DOCTOR,
  WEATHER
temporary → REPAIRS
tennis → SPORTS
tent → CAMPING AND
  CARAVANNING
tent peg → CAMPING AND
  CARAVANNING
tent pole → CAMPING AND
  CARAVANNING
terrace → EATING OUT
thank you → CONVERSATION –
  MEETING
that one → ORDERING
theatre → ENTERTAINMENT
thick → COLOURS AND SHAPES
thin → COLOURS AND SHAPES
third → MEASUREMENTS

this one → ORDERING
throat → BODY
through → DIRECTIONS
thumb → BODY
thunderstorm → WEATHER
ticket → CITY TRAVEL,
  ENTERTAINMENT, TRIPS AND
  EXCURSIONS
ticket collector → TRAIN TRAVEL
ticket office → RAILWAY
  STATION
tie → CLOTHES
tights → CLOTHES
till → PAYING
time → TIME, TIME PHRASES
timetable board → RAILWAY
  STATION
tin → FOOD – GENERAL
tinted → COLOURS AND SHAPES
tip, to → TIPPING
tissues → TOILETRIES
tobacco → CUSTOMS AND
  PASSPORTS
toe → BODY
toilet → TOILETS
toilet paper → TOILETS
toilet water → TOILETRIES
toll → DRIVING ABROAD
tomatoes → FOOD – FRUIT AND
  VEG
tomorrow → BUSINESS
tongue → BODY
tonight → NIGHTLIFE
too → CLOTHES
tooth → DENTIST
toothache → DENTIST
toothbrush → TOILETRIES
toothpaste → TOILETRIES
torch → USEFUL ITEMS

torn → REPAIRS
tour → TRIPS AND EXCURSIONS
tourist → DIRECTIONS
tourist office → MAPS AND GUIDES
tourist ticket → CITY TRAVEL
tow rope → BREAKDOWNS
tow, to → BREAKDOWNS
towel → BEACH, HAIRDRESSER'S
town → CITY TRAVEL
town centre → CITY TRAVEL
town plan → MAPS AND GUIDES
trade fair → BUSINESS
traffic → ROAD CONDITIONS
traffic jam → ROAD CONDITIONS
traffic lights → DRIVING ABROAD
traffic offence → POLICE
traffic warden → POLICE
trailer → CAMPING AND CARAVANNING
train → CITY TRAVEL, TRAIN TRAVEL
transfer charge call → TELEPHONE
transfer, to → MONEY
transit, in t. → LUGGAGE
travel, to → GIFTS AND SOUVENIRS
traveller's cheques → MONEY
trim → HAIRDRESSER'S
trip → SIGHTSEEING
tripod → PHOTOGRAPHY
trouble → PROBLEMS
trousers → CLOTHES
trunk → LUGGAGE
trunks → CLOTHES
try on, to → CLOTHES
tunnel → ROAD CONDITIONS

turn off, to → COMPLAINTS
turn on, to → COMPLAINTS
turn, to → TAXIS
turning → DIRECTIONS
turquoise → COLOURS AND SHAPES
TV lounge → HOTEL DESK
twice → MEASUREMENTS
tyre → CAR PARTS
tyre pressure → PETROL STATION
umbrella → USEFUL ITEMS
unconscious → DOCTOR
under → DIRECTIONS
underground → CITY TRAVEL
underground station → CITY TRAVEL
understand, to → ASKING QUESTIONS
unpleasant → DESCRIBING THINGS
upset → CHEMIST'S
urgently → DENTIST
use, to → TOILETS
vacancies → CAMPING AND CARAVANNING
vacuum cleaner → USEFUL ITEMS
veal → FOOD – GENERAL
vegetables → EATING OUT
vending machine → TOILETS
vermouth → WINES AND SPIRITS
vest → CLOTHES
view → SIGHTSEEING
vinegar → FOOD – GENERAL
visit → TRIPS AND EXCURSIONS
vodka → WINES AND SPIRITS
voltage → ROOM SERVICE
wait, to → COMPLAINTS, TAXIS

waiter → ORDERING
waiting room → RAILWAY
STATION
waitress → ORDERING
walk, to → DIRECTIONS
wallet → MONEY
warm → DESCRIBING THINGS,
WEATHER
warning triangle
→ BREAKDOWNS
wash off, to → CLEANING
washbasin → CLEANING,
TOILETS
washing powder → CLEANING
washing-up liquid → USEFUL
ITEMS
washroom → CAMPING AND
CARAVANNING
waste bin → TOILETS
watch → GIFTS AND SOUVENIRS
water → BEACH, EATING OUT,
PETROL STATION
water heater → SELF-CATERING
water-skiing → WATERSPORTS
way → DIRECTIONS
weak → DESCRIBING THINGS
weather → WEATHER
weather forecast → SAILING
wedding → CELEBRATIONS
week → CUSTOMS AND
PASSPORTS
well done → ORDERING
Welsh → PERSONAL DETAILS
wet → WEATHER
wetsuit → WATERSPORTS
wheel → CAR PARTS
wheel brace → BREAKDOWNS
white → COLOURS AND SHAPES,
WINES AND SPIRITS

white coffee → DRINKS
wife → PERSONAL DETAILS
wind → SAILING
window → SHOPPING, TRAIN
TRAVEL
window seat → AIRPORT
windscreen → CAR PARTS
windscreen washer → CAR
PARTS
windscreen wiper → CAR PARTS
windsurfing → WATERSPORTS
windy → WEATHER
wine → WINES AND SPIRITS
wine list → WINES AND SPIRITS
wool → CLOTHES
work, to → COMPLAINTS
wrap, to → BUYING
wrist → BODY
writing paper → STATIONERY
wrong → BUYING
wrong number → TELEPHONE
yellow → COLOURS AND SHAPES
yes → CONVERSATION –
MEETING
yoghurt → FOOD – GENERAL